W9-CEB-244

Roe v. Wade:
A WOMAN'S CHOICE?

SUPREME COURT MILESTONES

Roe v. Wade:

A WOMAN'S CHOICE?

SUSAN DUDLEY GOLD

BENCHMARK **B**OOKS

MARSHALL CAVENDISH

In memory of Beth Gallagher

*Dedicated to the members of "The Committee," my friends
Dorinne Spirito, Marilyn Stoesser-Casad, Gloria Wallace
Sheehan, and Maureen Leary, with deep gratitude for
their friendship and support through the years.*

*With special thanks to Professor David M. O'Brien of the Woodrow
Wilson Department of Politics at the University of Virginia for
reviewing the text of this book.*

Benchmark Books · Marshall Cavendish · 99 White Plains Road
Tarrytown, NY 10591 · www.marshallcavendish.us · Copyright © 2005 by Susan Dudley
Gold · All rights reserved. No part of this book may be reproduced or utilized in any form
or by any means electronic or mechanical including photocopying, recording, or by any
information storage and retrieval system, without permission from the copyright holders.

All Internet sites were available and accurate when sent to press.

Library of Congress Cataloging-in-Publication Data

Gold, Susan Dudley. Roe v. Wade : a women's choice? / by Susan Dudley Gold. · p. cm. —
(Supreme Court milestones) Includes bibliographical references and index. · Contents: Two
women's stories — Bans on abortion — A case and a plaintiff — Filing suit — Making a case
for abortion — Arguments — A momentous decision. · ISBN 0-7614-1839-3 · 1. Roe, Jane,
1947—-Trials, litigation, etc.—Juvenile literature. 2. Wade, Henry—Trials, litigation, etc.—
Juvenile literature. 3. Trials (Abortion)—United States—Juvenile literature. 4. Abortion—
Law and legislation—United States—Juvenile literature. [1. Roe, Jane, 1947—-Trials, litigation, etc. 2. Wade, Henry—Trials, litigation, etc. 3. Trials (Abortion) 4. Abortion—Law and
legislation.] I. Title: Roe versus Wade. II. Title. III. Series. · KF228.R59G647 2004 · 342.7308'
4—dc22 2003025567

Series design by Sonia Chaghatzbanian · Photo Research by Candlepants Incorporated
Printed in China · 3 5 6 4 2

Cover Photo: AFP/Corbis

The photographs in this book are used by permission and through the courtesy of: *Corbis*:
AFP, 1, 115,125; Mark Peterson, 2–3; Greg Smith/SABA, 6, 9; John Sprinnger Collection, 10;
Bettmann, 19, 44, 49, 86, 87, 97; Ted Streshinsky, 34; Wally McNamee, 88; *AP/Wide World
Photos*: 14, 31, 52, 72, 95. *Reproduced with Permission from Planned Parenthood®
Federation of America, Inc. All Rights Reserved*: 25; *Randy Eli Grothe/Dallas Morning News*:
60, 62; *Irwin Schwar*: 66; *Sarah Weddington*: 75, 92; *Photograph by Robert Oakes/National
Geographic/Collection of the Supreme Court of The United States*: 78; *Sarah Standiford*: 102;
Silent No More/Photo by Stephen Bartling: 107.

contents

PRO-CHOICE DEMONSTRATORS AND POLICE GUARD THE ENTRANCE TO THE WOMEN'S CARE CENTER IN 1994 AS AN ANTIABORTION PROTESTER KNEELS ON THE LAWN.

Introduction
A Fundamental Right

ON JANUARY 22, 1973, the U.S. Supreme Court ruled that a woman has a constitutional right to abort a pregnancy. According to the ruling, states and the federal government can ban abortion only in the last three months of a woman's pregnancy.

Known as *Roe* v. *Wade*, the sweeping decision said the abortion right is as fundamental as the right to vote or the right to free speech. It struck down antiabortion laws in thirty-one states and required eighteen more to rewrite theirs. Only New York state's liberal law, which allowed women to have abortions without restrictions, remained unaffected by the decision.

Most Supreme Court decisions serve as the final word on a matter. People may object to a ruling, but eventually they accept that a particular decision has become the law of the land. That has not happened with *Roe* v. *Wade*. Far from putting the matter to rest, the abortion decision ignited the bitter battle between those who oppose abortion and those who support a woman's right to control her own body.

The protest against abortion turned violent in the late-1980s and early 1990s. A few extreme antiabortion groups began bombing abortion clinics and killing doctors and staff members. Hecklers intimidated women seeking treatment at abortion clinics. This atmosphere of violence made it harder for women to get an abortion. Fewer doctors were willing to face the danger; women were reluctant to cross picket lines and endure insults and threats.

Actions by state and federal officials have also limited women's access to abortion. Congress has eliminated funding for abortions for most women employed by the government, including members of the military, and for poor women whose health care costs are paid by Medicaid. State legislators continue to pass laws to put restrictions on abortions. Some of those laws—but not all—have won support from the Supreme Court. Judicial support for abortion rights has narrowed, as antiabortion judges take their place on the Supreme Court and lower courts.

The battle continues as those supporting *Roe* work to keep a woman's right to an abortion intact, while those opposed continue efforts to overturn the ruling.

Antiabortion demonstrators conduct a sit-in to block the entrance of the Women's Care Center pregnancy clinic in Little Rock, Arkansas, in 1994.

Actress Polly Bergen in 1953. An illegal abortion she had when she was a teenager scarred her so badly she was never able to have a child.

one
TWO WOMEN'S STORIES

POLLY Bergen—living with a roommate in Hollywood and earning barely enough as a singer to pay the rent—was just seventeen when she got pregnant. She knew she did not want to have a baby. The man involved had broken off the relationship, and she feared her parents would be destroyed if they knew the truth. It was 1947, and society treated unmarried mothers harshly.

With help from her roommate, she found a man who performed abortions. Bergen, who became a noted actress, recalled the ordeal in *The Choices We Made*, a collection of stories on abortion by twenty-five women and men. She went alone to the Los Angeles address she had been given. A man answered the door and asked for the three-hundred-dollar fee. She handed him the money, which she had borrowed from friends who did not know the real reason she needed it.

"I was very scared," she said, remembering that day. She lay on a table wrapped in a sheet while the man used a sharp instrument to cut her. He gave her no anesthesia, although the surgery was "extremely painful," Bergen said. Many abortionists did not use painkillers or anesthesia because patients would have had to stay longer and could have had problems that could not be handled outside a hospital. Abortions were illegal, and the abortionist could go to jail if caught.

After the procedure, Bergen went to her apartment and stayed in bed for three days. There was so much blood she thought she was dying. When her roommate came home, she took her to a doctor who probably saved her life. Years later she found out that the abortionist had scarred her so badly that she would never be able to have a child.

As painful as the experience was for Bergen, she fared better than some women in similar circumstances. Other young women died from botched abortions. In some cases, hospitals and doctors refused to treat women who had had illegal abortions.

A survey conducted by Alfred Kinsey for his 1953 groundbreaking book *Sexual Behavior in the Human Female* showed that abortions took place far more often than the number of board-approved operations indicated. Kinsey's poll revealed that nine of ten unmarried women who became pregnant had abortions and 22 percent of married women ended at least one of their pregnancies.

In the 1960s, experts estimated that one million American women obtained abortions each year. Botched operations claimed the lives of an estimated five thousand to ten thousand of these women annually. Thousands more suffered severe medical problems caused by unsanitary conditions, infections, and other health risks related to illegal abortions.

Most of these deaths and injuries went unnoticed by the press and the public. Families hushed up the real cause of death to protect their loved ones. Women seeking abortions often kept their conditions secret, even from their closest family members. It took a highly publicized case to bring the issue out into the open.

SHERRI FINKBINE'S ORDEAL

A cold panic gripped Sherri Finkbine when she read the newspaper story. Several babies had been born in

England with just heads and torsos—no arms or legs. Doctors believed the tragedy had occurred because the babies' mothers had taken sleeping pills during the early part of their pregnancies. The doctors blamed a drug called thalidomide for the deformities.

Finkbine loved children. Known as Sherri Chessen on TV, she hosted the children's show *Romper Room*, delighting her preschool audience. The Phoenix, Arizona, resident also was the mother of four children and was pregnant with her fifth child.

She thought back to the pills she had taken during the first months of her pregnancy when morning sickness had plagued her. Her husband, Robert Finkbine, a high-school history teacher, had brought the pills home from England, where he had led his students on a school trip. An English doctor had prescribed the pills when Robert Finkbine had trouble sleeping.

Thinking the pills would calm her and help her nausea, Sherri Finkbine took about three dozen of the pills over the next two months. Now, reading the paper on this July morning in 1962, she thought apprehensively that the pills she had taken sounded suspiciously like the ones that had caused the deformities.

Shaken by fear, she called her doctor and described the pills to him. They did indeed contain thalidomide, he told her. Even worse, the drug was most destructive to fetuses in the first three months of pregnancy. She asked what she should do. The doctor recommended an abortion.

In Arizona in 1962, abortions were legal only if they were performed to save the life of the mother. In Phoenix, doctors performed between eighteen and twenty-five legal abortions a year. Before an abortion was performed, a panel of doctors had to determine that the birth would endanger the mother's life.

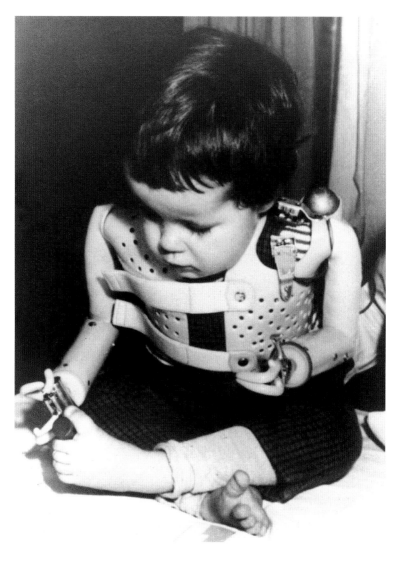

CHILDREN LIKE THIS ONE, WHOSE MOTHERS TOOK THALIDOMIDE, A COMMONLY PRESCRIBED SLEEPING PILL IN THE 1950S AND EARLY 1960S, WERE BORN WITH SEVERE DEFORMITIES.

During the first three months of a woman's pregnancy, doctors used a device to suck the fetus from the mother's womb. If the woman was more than three months pregnant, doctors had to operate to remove the fetus.

Finkbine, thirty, was almost two and a half months pregnant when she learned she had taken thalidomide. An abortion performed at this stage would be a simple medical procedure. Once she was more than three months pregnant she would have to have surgery, a more complicated and dangerous undertaking.

Reassured by her doctor, Finkbine sent a note to the three-doctor medical board at the hospital where she sought an abortion. She explained her situation and requested that she be given an abortion as soon as possible. The panel recommended to the hospital that the abortion be performed. Her doctor scheduled the procedure for the following Thursday.

Then, hoping to prevent other mothers from taking thalidomide, Finkbine called the editor of a Phoenix newspaper. By this time, four thousand deformed babies whose mothers had taken thalidomide had been reported in Germany and another thousand in England, Canada, and Australia. The babies were born with flipperlike arms and legs. In some cases, their hands and feet were attached directly to their bodies. Though the drug had been banned in the United States in March 1962, it had been distributed since 1959 to more than 1,200 doctors throughout the country for tests on patients. Other Americans had obtained the drug abroad, as had Robert Finkbine.

Sherri Finkbine told her story to a medical reporter, asking that her name not be used. The next day, a front-page story blared out her tragedy: "Baby-deforming Drug May Cost Woman Her Child Here." In the next few days, the story was carried by newspapers throughout the world.

Though the newspapers honored Finkbine's request not to publish her name, the media spotlight on Phoenix and its hospitals did not sit well with the medical community. Afraid they would be prosecuted for violating Arizona's abortion law, the hospital and doctors cancelled Finkbine's abortion.

Her doctor told her, "It is now a legal decision. It's no longer a medical or humanitarian one, I'm afraid."

The Finkbines decided to take their case to court. On July 25, 1962, they filed suit in superior court, asking the judge to declare Arizona's 1901 abortion law illegal. Stephen Morris, administrator of the Good Samaritan Hospital, where the abortion had been scheduled, joined their suit. The hospital was willing to perform the abortion if the courts ruled that the action would be legal.

Once the court documents were filed, the Finkbines' names became public. Newspapers nationwide now recorded every move they made. *The New York Times* reported that Sherri Finkbine had talked to two psychiatrists in an effort to show that the birth would endanger her life. "It would upset me terribly to have a deformed baby," she said, noting that her mental health would be affected.

While they waited for a court judgment, the Finkbines read about three babies born deformed in New York City. Their deformities were blamed on thalidomide.

On July 29, the Finkbines' attorney offered to drop the court suit if the state would guarantee it would not prosecute if the abortion were performed. The state would not give such an assurance.

The following day, Judge Yale McFate dismissed the Finkbines' case without a hearing. He said there was no legal controversy or dispute because all sides in the case agreed to the facts as presented by the Finkbines.

"As a human being I would like to hear the case," Judge McFate told the Finkbines. "As a judge, under existing Arizona law, I cannot."

Time was running short. Sherri Finkbine's pregnancy was progressing. The longer an abortion was delayed, the more dangerous it became. Meanwhile, *The New York Times* reported that a New York woman who had taken thalidomide had given birth to a baby whose internal organs and all four limbs were deformed. The baby lived forty-one minutes.

The Finkbines desperately searched for a place where Sherri Finkbine could obtain a legal abortion. In 1962, aborting a fetus was a felony in every state unless the life of the mother (or her health in some cases) was endangered. Alabama, the District of Columbia, and Oregon allowed abortions to preserve the mother's health. Maryland doctors had to prove an abortion was necessary for the mother's safety. In Colorado and New Mexico, an abortion was permitted to "prevent permanent bodily injury" to the mother. But there had been few court rulings to define "health," "safety," or "permanent bodily injury."

No one seemed to be able to give the Finkbines a clear answer about the legality of the abortion they sought. On July 31, Robert Finkbine told *The New York Times* of the couple's decision to seek an abortion outside the country. They chose to go to a country where abortion was legal because they did not want to break the law, he told news reporters.

At the time, seven countries permitted abortions: Japan, Finland, Norway, England, Sweden, Denmark, and the Soviet Union. The Finkbines' doctor recommended Japan, where those seeking abortions paid as little as fifty dollars and encountered little red tape. Because of the publicity surrounding the Finkbines' case, however, the Japanese government was reluctant to allow Sherri Finkbine to undergo an abortion there.

Instead, the Finkbines decided to go to Sweden. A medical journalist from Sweden offered to arrange an appointment for Sherri Finkbine with a Swedish doctor. They booked a flight to Sweden on August 3.

That same day, the Vatican broadcast a proclamation condemning those who sought abortions, even if the pregnancy threatened the mother's life. "Every human being, from the first instant of conception, possesses all the rights that belong to any human person," the broadcast said. "Nothing justifies direct, voluntary suppression—not even the goal of saving the life of the mother."

The radio broadcast did not mention the Finkbines by name, but Boston's auxiliary bishop, Thomas J. Riley, did. He likened Sherri Finkbine's hoped-for abortion to "killing an innocent boy or girl."

Other religious leaders, however, expressed a different view. Dr. Theodore R. Flaiz, world medical director of the Seventh Day Adventist Church, called the Finkbine abortion "therapeutic." Protestant and Jewish religious leaders in the Finkbines' home state had not opposed the operation. The Finkbines' church, the Unitarian Universalist Association, had long been in the forefront of working for abortion reform.

In Sweden Sherri Finkbine had to follow the same lengthy procedures Swedish women had to endure to

SHERRI FINKBINE STANDS OUTSIDE THE ROYAL CAROLINE HOSPITAL IN
STOCKHOLM, SWEDEN, WHERE DOCTORS PERFORMED AN ABORTION ON HER ON
AUGUST 18, 1962. SHE HAD TO GO TO SWEDEN FOR THE OPERATION BECAUSE NO
U.S. HOSPITAL WOULD PERFORM THE PROCEDURE. WHILE PREGNANT,
FINKBINE HAD TAKEN A MEDICATION CALLED THALIDOMIDE THAT CAUSED
THE FETUS TO BE DEFORMED.

obtain an abortion. She spent the next few days being examined and interviewed by social workers, psychiatrists, and an obstetrician. After completing the examinations, Finkbine submitted her application to the three-person Royal Medical Board of Sweden.

The board, composed of a gynecologist, a psychiatrist, and a woman specialist in social and political questions, made the final decision on whether to grant abortions in Sweden. The operation was permitted if the mother's health or life were in danger, the birth would affect the mother's "physical or psychic health," the mother was under fifteen or had been raped, or the mother would pass along genetic defects to the child.

The board approved Finkbine's request in order to safeguard her "mental health." Doctors at the Royal Caroline Hospital in Stockholm, Sweden, performed an abortion on Finkbine August 18, 1962—almost a month after she had learned the fetus she carried might be deformed. They estimated she was in her thirteenth week of pregnancy. The fetus was deformed.

Robert Finkbine told reporters that he and his wife both thought it was "wonderful" that there was a country where abortions were "a medical decision, not obstructed by religious, legal, and social pressures."

On her return to the United States, relieved to have the experience behind her, Mrs. Finkbine told the press, "The Swedish people are the most intelligent, understanding in the world. Americans try to hide their heads in the sand like an ostrich and hope such problems will go away."

She later wrote, "An abortion was to me a very sad, ugly experience, but [it was] definitely the lesser of two evils."

The producers of *Romper Room* replaced Sherri Finkbine on the show because of the publicity over her ordeal. During and after the tragedy, the family received death threats from people opposed to abortion.

TWO
BANS ON ABORTION

THE FINKBINE TRAGEDY convinced many people there was a need for more liberal abortion laws in the United States. The Finkbines had been able to go to Sweden for an abortion, but many others could not afford such a trip. The birth of the "thalidomide babies" and a 1962 to 1965 epidemic of German measles in the United States that led to deformed fetuses disturbed people. Health professionals and many others began calling for legalized abortions when the baby might be born with physical or mental defects.

For the next decade, however, women who wanted abortions would be forced to seek the services of illegal abortionists if their case did not fit into the law's narrow loopholes. For poor women, the laws offered no other option since they could not afford the costs involved.

Although well-entrenched in twentieth-century America, the ban on abortion had been only fairly recently established as law. The Greeks and Romans used abortion as an accepted method of limiting the size of their families. That attitude prevailed in much of England and other countries of Europe and their colonies through the 1700s. In the American colonies and later in the newly formed United States, abortion in the early months of pregnancy was left to the discretion of the mother. Even in the later months of pregnancy, abortion was viewed as little more than a misdemeanor.

THE FIRST ABORTION LAWS

Not until the nineteenth century did states begin to adopt laws regulating abortion, although they did so to protect the mother, not the fetus. During the early 1800s, 30 percent of the women undergoing abortions in New York died from infections following the procedure.

The first such law, adopted by Connecticut in 1821, made it illegal to give pregnant women poison to induce abortion. This was a common method at the time and one that was often fatal to both fetus and mother. The Connecticut law and others that followed applied only to mothers who had reached the "quickening" stage, the point when a woman can feel the fetus moving inside her (usually around the twentieth week for a first pregnancy).

As the Industrial Revolution swept the country in the late 1800s, the need for large families declined. People moved from farms and rural areas to the cities. Farmers began to use machines to do much of the work they had once done by hand. Mills and factories enticed a growing number of women to enter the work force to supplement their families' incomes. These women, working at jobs outside the home, tended to have fewer babies per family. Between 1800 and 1900, the average number of children born to white American women decreased from 7.04 to 3.56. During this time, abortions became more common, and women turned to home remedies, such as plants and soap solutions. By the mid-1800s, one in five pregnancies ended in abortion, according to some estimates.

Many men of the late nineteenth century saw the early women's movement and the rising number of women laborers as a threat to their power. They believed that a woman's role in life should revolve only around being a mother. Abortion, they believed, worked against what they viewed as the natural order of things. An American Medical Association (AMA) report on abortion issued in 1871 reflected that view. It described a woman who had an abortion as "unmindful of the course marked out for her by Providence."

The U.S. Congress reinforced this image of women when it passed the Comstock Act in 1873. The act banned the distribution of information about abortion and birth control. Congress passed the law to "enforce chastity on the young and unmarried and to preserve the position of women within the traditional family structure."

The push to make abortion a crime came largely from the medical community. The newly organized AMA had several reasons for wanting to make abortions illegal. First, doctors feared for the safety of women who had abortions performed by unskilled practitioners or who tried to perform abortions on themselves. The medical profession also wanted to exert control over medical procedures. Licensed doctors believed they, not untrained practitioners, should be the ones to administer abortions. In addition, many doctors believed abortions were immoral and thought they should be banned.

The AMA lobbied state legislatures to ban abortion and used newspaper articles to sway public opinion against the procedure. One physician, Horatio Storer, circulated flyers noting that more Protestant than

MARGARET SANGER, WHO REVOLUTIONIZED FEMALE CONTRACEPTION, SPEAK-
ING TO A GROUP OF SUPPORTERS IN FAVOR OF OVERTURNING THE COMSTOCK
ACT OF 1873, WHICH MADE IT ILLEGAL TO DISTRIBUTE INFORMATION ABOUT
ABORTION AND BIRTH CONTROL.

Catholic women had abortions. These tracts fanned
fears among some Protestants that Catholic immigrants
would soon outnumber them.

The AMA campaign successfully turned society
against abortion. During the last quarter of the 1800s,
more than forty states and territories passed laws banning
abortion. Exceptions were made to save the mother's life,
but most laws required that at least one doctor state the
abortion was necessary. With the passage of these laws,

the decision to have an abortion had effectively been removed from the woman's control and placed under the doctor's authority.

ILLeGaL ABOrTIONS CLAIM LIVeS

Despite the widespread ban on abortion, women continued to find ways to undergo the procedure. As many as one in three pregnancies ended in abortion during the early twentieth century, according to some experts. Rich, well-established women merely found a doctor willing to perform an abortion. Other women were forced to abort illegally through their own devices or at back-alley abortion mills. Often the illegal abortion clinics were no more than dirty rooms operated by untrained staff. Many women died at the hands of unskilled abortionists.

By the mid-1900s, many doctors had changed their stance on abortion. They once again led efforts to change attitudes about abortion—this time in favor of liberalizing the laws. Concerned over the numbers of women they saw injured and killed by illegal abortions, they sought to make abortions legal and thus move the procedure from the back alleys to sterile hospitals. Abortions done by skilled doctors under modern conditions had become as safe or safer than childbirth.

Doctors saw deformed babies born as the result of genetic defects, drugs such as thalidomide, and exposure to diseases such as German measles. Many doctors came to believe, as Sherri Finkbine did, that abortion was less repugnant than bringing a severely deformed baby into the world.

Doctors favoring the reform of abortion laws joined

forces with women's groups and members of the clergy. Dr. Robert E. Hall, an assistant professor of obstetrics and gynecology at Columbia University's College of Physicians and Surgeons, noted in 1965 that, because of advances in modern medicine, pregnancy rarely threatened the life of the average American woman. Women were more likely to suffer ill health or give birth to deformed fetuses, he said. The New York abortion law, which permitted abortions only to save the life of the mother, was "inhumane and unrealistic," Dr. Hall said, because it failed to address the more common risks facing women.

As head of the Association for Humane Abortion, Dr. Hall sent questionnaires to New York obstetricians in 1965 asking about their views on abortion. Of the 1,372 who answered, 87 percent said they favored changes in the eighty-three-year-old law. They supported a model law that had been proposed in 1959 by the American Law Institute (ALI). The ALI, a respected group of legal scholars, had recommended that the Model Penal Code allow abortions in cases of rape, if the fetus was deformed, or if two doctors stated that the woman's health would be harmed by continuing her pregnancy. The organization presents its proposals for criminal law on a regular basis as a guide for legislators. Previous model laws proposed by ALI had allowed abortion only to save the mother's life.

In 1967, New York Governor Nelson Rockefeller called for revisions to that state's abortion law. *The New York Times* ran editorials that year urging the legislature to change the law. A National Opinion Research Center poll revealed that a majority of Americans, including Catholics, supported liberalized abortion laws.

VARYING VIEWS AMONG RELIGIOUS LEADERS

During the late 1960s, most of the opposition to abortion came from the Roman Catholic Church. In January 1967, a group with ties to the Catholic Church called the Right to Life Committee was formed to fight proposed changes in the New York State abortion law. The Church said the procedure was "contrary to moral law" and forbade its parishioners to have abortions even to save the life of the mother. On Sunday, February 12, 1967, priests throughout New York State read a pastoral letter to their Catholic congregations urging them to fight the legislature's efforts to modify the law. Some Orthodox Jews and Fundamentalist Protestant groups joined the antiabortion movement.

Other religious groups, however, took opposite stands on abortion. In 1963, the General Assembly of the Unitarian Universalist Association passed a resolution calling the nation's restrictive abortion laws an "affront to human life and dignity." Four years later, the Archbishop of Canterbury, the spiritual leader of the Anglican Church, called for legalized abortion in Great Britain when the mental or physical health of the mother was in danger, there was a risk of a deformed child, or the pregnancy was the result of rape.

The Young Women's Christian Association (YWCA), the United Church of Christ, the United Methodist Church, the United Presbyterian Church, and the Episcopal Church all lent support to the efforts to make abortion legal in New York.

On May 22, 1967, New York City rabbis and Protestant ministers announced the formation of the Clergy Consultation Service on Abortion. Appearing on the front page of *The New York Times*, the story detailed the religious leaders' intention of helping women obtain safe abortions. By the early 1970s, the group had opened counseling services in most major cities. The counselors referred women to doctors willing to perform safe abortions. The clergy's actions showed that the effort to ease abortion laws was firmly rooted in mainstream America.

It was also becoming obvious that for a growing number of people—including white, middle-class women—abortion was an acceptable alternative to unwanted pregnancy. Many of these women could get an abortion at their doctor's office. Some doctors provided abortions out of compassion and the desire to serve their patients. Some did it for the money. An article in the *Atlantic Monthly* written in 1965 by an anonymous woman illustrates the relative ease with which some women could find an abortionist. When her own doctor refused to do the procedure, the writer called five friends and got referrals to four different doctors plus an abortion service in a neighboring state. She chose one of the doctors and, after paying five hundred dollars, had the abortion with only minor medical symptoms. She concluded that many other women followed the same route.

She wrote:

I am sure that my experience is not unique. There must be hundreds like me from coast to coast who for sober and considered reasons daily undergo the same fears, search for the same kinds of operative sources, and find the money necessary to terminate unwanted pregnancy.

support grows for liberal laws

On June 22, 1967, in another front-page story in *The New York Times*, the American Medical Association's House of Delegates declared its support for liberalized abortion laws. It was the first time since 1871 that the doctors' group had changed its position on abortion.

Women's rights groups gained momentum during this time. They began to focus on women's health issues and their goal for women to make their own decisions about their bodies and medical treatment. As part of this approach, these groups took a harder stand on abortion, fighting to repeal—not just reform—abortion laws throughout the country. Unlike earlier efforts by doctors and politicians, this campaign called for women—not medical staff—to determine when to have an abortion. In 1962, Pat Maginnis and other women founded the Society for Humane Abortion in San Francisco, California. Urging the repeal of all abortion laws, the group distributed information about birth control and abortion to women across the nation. The members' efforts spurred women in other communities to form similar groups and support the repeal movement.

Betty Friedan and other activists believed a national organization to fight for women's rights was necessary. Their efforts led to the formation of the National Organization for Women (NOW) in 1966. At its national conference the next year, NOW included the "Right of Women to Control their Reproductive Lives" in its Women's Bill of Rights.

Some women activists took direct action to help women seeking abortions. In Chicago, the Abortion Counseling Service of Women's Liberation ran an

BETTY FRIEDAN WAS A LEADER OF THE FEMINIST MOVEMENT IN THE 1960S. HER
EFFORTS, AND THOSE OF LIKE-MINDED FEMINISTS, LED TO THE FORMATION OF
THE NATIONAL ORGANIZATION FOR WOMEN (NOW) IN 1966. ONE OF NOW'S
KEY ISSUES WAS THE RIGHT OF WOMEN TO CONTROL THEIR REPRODUCTIVE LIVES.

underground operation that provided low-cost abortions by doctors willing to do the procedure. The service, founded in 1969 to make abortions safe and available to poor women and teenage girls, used the code name Jane. In the beginning, the organization hired medical professionals to perform the abortions. When a man who had been doing the abortions turned out not to be a medical doctor as the group had thought, the women decided they, too, could learn to perform the operation safely. The abortionist trained them, and for four years the women conducted the abortions in their homes. By doing the operations themselves, they were able to reduce the fee to no more than one hundred dollars. Poor women often paid nothing. Abortions performed by doctors could cost as much as a thousand dollars.

Women's rights advocates joined forces with doctors and lawyers to form the National Association for the Repeal of Abortion Laws (NARAL) in 1969. NARAL devoted all of its energies to the repeal effort. The organization served as a major lobbyist for repeal and worked with state legislators to erase abortion laws from the books. NARAL also challenged abortion laws in court.

Organizations such as Planned Parenthood Federation of America, the YWCA, and groups concerned with overpopulation joined women activists in the battle to repeal abortion laws. Well-established professional organizations also added their weight to the effort. In 1968 the American Public Health Association called for safe and legal abortions for all women seeking them. In February 1971 the American Bar Association voted in favor of allowing abortion up to the twentieth week of pregnancy. The following month, the Commission on Population Growth and the American Future issued a report to Congress recommending that states allow doctors to give abortions to all women who asked for them. The report also urged the federal government to pay for abortion services and proposed that birth control devices be made available to teens.

CHANGING STATE LAWS

Advocates for changing abortion laws focused their efforts on two arenas: state legislatures and the courts. State lawmakers responded to the pressure by slowly expanding the circumstances under which women could have legal abortions. A few states added endangerment of the mother's health and risk of having a deformed child to the reasons for a legal abortion. In 1967, Governor John Love of Colorado signed into law a bill that permitted abortions for those reasons and in the case of rape or incest. To obtain a legal abortion under Colorado law, however, a pregnant woman had to win the approval of a panel of three doctors.

California passed a similar bill in 1967. It permitted abortions when the mother's health was "gravely threatened." Governor Ronald Reagan "reluctantly" signed the bill, which did not require a mother to live in California to obtain an abortion there.

By 1970, twelve states had passed liberal abortion bills. Many more legislatures were considering bills that would make it easier to obtain abortions in their states. Even with the reforms, however, hundreds of thousands of American women continued to undergo illegal abortions. In California, an estimated 100,000 women had illegal abortions each year, while only two thousand abortions were performed

CALIFORNIA PASSED A LAW IN 1967 THAT PERMITTED ABORTIONS WHEN THE MOTHER'S HEALTH WAS AT GREAT RISK. GOVERNOR RONALD REAGAN RELUCTANTLY SIGNED THE LEGISLATION; AS PRESIDENT, HE SUPPORTED ANTIABORTION FORCES.

legally during the six months after the state's new law went into effect.

Price, access to medical care, and abortion laws' restrictions all played a role in whether women resorted to illegal abortions. To obtain an abortion legally, women still had to fit certain guidelines set by the laws in their states. In most of the "reform" states, women had to convince a panel of doctors that childbirth would endanger their health or that they met the law's requirements in other ways.

Certification by psychiatrists or physicians was expensive, as was a hospital abortion. Charges could run as high as $700 (more than $3,300 in 2003 dollars), while an illegal abortion might cost only $200 (around $950 in 2003 dollars). Women in search of abortions often had to travel long distances to states with more relaxed abortion laws. The trips added to the cost of the abortions and meant that teenagers, the poor, and rural women seldom had access to legal abortions.

Hawaii became the first state to repeal its abortion law and allow abortions during the early months of a pregnancy. Under the law, passed in 1970, women could have abortions for any reason, but the procedure had to be performed in a hospital. The law applied only to residents of Hawaii.

New York soon followed with an even more liberal law. In introducing the bill that would repeal the state's 1830 abortion law, Republican Assemblywoman Constance Cook noted the hypocrisy of the present ban on abortion, which had little effect on the wealthy but resulted in injury and death among the poor who sought abortions. "If a woman has money, she can go abroad," Cook told the Assembly. "If she has twenty-five dollars, she will get [an abortion] here, under abominable conditions. If she doesn't have twenty-five dollars, she can, of course, induce abortion herself."

The legislation passed by one vote, cast by Democrat George Michaels, after a bitter battle between the repeal forces and those opposed to abortion. The new legislation allowed abortions for any reason up to the twenty-fourth week of pregnancy. The law did not limit abortions to New York residents. The New York law, the most liberal in the nation, became the standard by which other efforts to lift abortion bans were judged.

one man's vote
made a difference

The dramatic battle over New York's abortion law demonstrated how one vote could change the course of history. It also pointed out how political careers could be won or lost based solely on an abortion vote.

In 1970 Republican Assemblywoman Constance Cook introduced a landmark bill to repeal the 1830 law that banned abortion in New York. The old law allowed the procedure only to save the mother's life. Cook's bill would allow abortion without restriction up to the twenty-fourth month of pregnancy. Abortion rights activists had tried unsuccessfully for four years to lift the state's ban on abortion.

After five hours of heated debate, the State Senate passed—on a 31 to 26 vote—a more liberal bill to lift the ban entirely. The Assembly—which acts as a house of representatives in New York—voted against Cook's bill but scheduled another vote on April 9, 1970. The week before the vote, the members of the Assembly endured intense pressure from the Catholic Church and other antiabortion supporters. More than one member changed his or her position on the bill after heavy lobbying from proponents and opponents of the measure. One member said his parish priest had described him and fellow supporters of the bill as "murderers" during a church service the member attended with his young daughter. Another said his church had printed his name in the parish newspaper as one "who acted improperly."

Republican Governor Nelson Rockefeller had pledged to sign the bill if it made it through the legislature. Since the Senate had already voted to repeal the old law, the final decision rested with the Assembly.

Assemblyman George Michaels, a Democrat with a conservative voting record, personally favored easing restrictions on abortions but knew many of his supporters— a large portion of whom were Catholics—vehemently opposed the bill. A fifty-nine-year-old lawyer serving his fifth term in the Assembly, Michaels had voted against changes in the abortion law in the past.

Michaels agonized over the bill. One of his sons had told him of the women he had seen mutilated and dying from botched abortions in the Cincinnati ghetto where he worked during his internship to become a rabbi. Like many in the Assembly, Michaels knew the vote would be close, but he assumed the bill would pass. When his daughter-in-law Sarah asked what he would do if the bill needed his vote to pass, he said he planned to vote against it anyway. The bill, he told her, would be reintroduced in the next session, two years later. "And how many women will be mutilated and die in that time?" she asked. The comment affected him deeply, said another of his sons. Although he, too, supported abortion rights, his son believed his father had to vote against the bill to keep his seat.

On the day of the vote, the bill's supporters took a quick count and thought they had just enough votes to win. With 150 members in the Assembly, the bill needed 76 votes to pass. The Republican Speaker of the House, Perry Duryea, had already promised to vote for the bill if his vote was needed. One member, a Democrat, was absent.

Finally, after four hours of debate, the Assembly prepared to vote on the bill. The room was tense as the roll call began. George Michaels cast a no vote, as he had pledged to do. It looked as if the bill would pass when Anthony Stella, a Democratic Assemblyman from the Bronx who had voted to support the bill the previous week, reversed his position. He said he had changed his vote because of pressure from his Catholic constituents. Supporters of the bill who knew Michaels' personal views pleaded with him to reconsider his position. Without Michaels' vote, the bill would fail.

As the final vote was cast and the clerk prepared to announce the bill's defeat, George Michaels quietly stood. Hands trembling and tears in his eyes, Michaels said he was switching his vote from no to yes. "I realize, Mr. Speaker," he said in a quavering voice, "that I am terminating my political career, but I cannot in good conscience sit here and allow my vote to be the one that defeats this bill. . . . What's the use of getting elected, or reelected, if you don't stand for something?"

Pandemonium erupted as Duryea added his vote and the clerk announced the bill's passage. Supporters sobbed with joy, clapping and cheering. Michaels, head down, felt the weight of what he had done bearing down on him. The final tally, 76 (including the speaker's yes vote) to 73, sent the bill to the Senate, which approved the Assembly version. Governor Rockefeller signed the bill into law, and New York became the first in the nation to allow unrestricted abortions during the first twenty-four weeks of pregnancy. The New York reforms became law on July 1, 1970. On July 2, the Syracuse Planned Parenthood opened its first abortion clinic, and women from all over the country began traveling to New York to get legal abortions.

Outraged at Michaels' action, the Democrats in Cayooga County held an emergency meeting later that April and voted to support a pro-life candidate in the upcoming primary. While on the campaign trail, Michaels nearly lost his life in a car accident. He spent the remaining days of the campaign in the hospital and lost the election.

Although Michaels received some hate mail, he got many more letters from grateful women and their relatives and friends. After recuperating, he ran a successful law firm in Auburn, New York, with his son Lee.

Lee Michaels said his father, who died of cancer in 1992, never regretted his vote even though it ended his political career. With a son's pride, Lee Michaels told how his father joined the marines at age thirty-one to fight in World War II when Lee was only one year old, how he spent countless hours working for constituents as an assemblyman, and how he served as a "fearless trial lawyer" representing clients.

"He was the bravest person I ever knew."

Several other states considered similar legislation. Maryland's General Assembly repealed that state's abortion laws in 1970, but Governor Marvin Mandel vetoed the action. Alaska's Governor Keith H. Miller did the same in his state, but the legislature there later overturned the veto. In each case, the legislative wrangling demonstrated the deeply held convictions by those on both sides of the question and the role politics played in the abortion issue.

The pro-choice forces—as abortion rights activists called themselves—began making major gains. By the end of 1970, Alaska had joined New York and Hawaii in repealing laws that banned abortions during the first months of pregnancy. Washington State repealed its abortion law the following year, and nineteen other states liberalized their abortion laws by the end of 1973.

At first pro-lifers—the term used by those against abortion—lacked the organization of the pro-choice groups. Most opposition came from the Catholic Church and grass-roots campaigns. During efforts to ease abortion laws in Pennsylvania in 1970, pro-life Representative Martin Mullen complained that those against abortion had not campaigned hard enough for their position. "You pro-lifers don't give me enough support," he said, pleading with them to "send letters. . . . Come to Harrisburg [the capital] . . . Let us know where you stand."

Nevertheless, pro-lifers continued to resist changes in the laws. The Roman Catholic Church, which had taken the lead in the effort to stop abortion, pushed to organize the movement. Countering moves to relax New York's abortion laws, Bishop James T. McHugh helped organize local antiabortion groups in that state. The first statewide group formed in 1967 as the Virginia

Society for Human Life, followed shortly by the New York State Right to Life Committee. In 1968, New Jersey lawyer Juan Ryan led the effort to establish a national organization, the National Right to Life Committee. Although the group began at a Catholic conference, the resulting organization called on people of all faiths to join the antiabortion campaign. In May 1973, the NRLC incorporated as a nonprofit, nondenominational group. It would become the leader in the pro-life movement.

On the national level, Senator Bob Packwood (R-Oregon) introduced a bill to lift the ban on abortion nationwide, but Congress failed to act on the proposal. In the 1968 presidential elections, Republican Richard Nixon supported the rights of fetuses, while Democrat George McGovern said the matter of abortion should be decided by a woman and her doctor. But the issue played little role in Nixon's ultimate landslide victory.

court battles

The push to legalize abortion met with more success on another front—the courts. In 1969, Federal District Judge Gerhard Gesell struck down a Washington, D.C., law that prohibited doctors from performing abortions except when the mother's health or life was in danger. Dr. Milan Vuitch, arrested by district police for performing illegal abortions, had appealed his conviction to the federal court. In his ruling in the case, *United States* v. *Vuitch*, Judge Gesell said the district law was unconstitutionally vague and suggested Congress rewrite it to make it apply to specific circumstances. The law did not define what was meant by "health" and did not address whether psychological factors should be considered in addition to physical health problems. The Supreme Court later upheld the law.

Encouraged by Judge Gesell's ruling, abortion rights activists decided they might have better luck in the courts than in individual state legislatures. In late 1969, the Center for Constitutional Rights—a New York-based group that uses the court system to safeguard individual rights—filed suit against New York's antiabortion law. In *Abramowicz* v. *Lefkowitz*, the group used testimony from dozens of women who described the agonies, health problems, and disruptions in their lives forced upon them by unwanted pregnancies. The suit, the first to present the issue from the viewpoint of women, asserted that the right to an abortion was fundamental. It based part of its claims on the right to privacy— a claim that would later be stated in *Roe* v. *Wade*. When New York repealed its abortion law, the case was dismissed, but it served as a model for other legal action.

In several states, the American Civil Liberties Union (ACLU)—an organization formed to protect people's constitutional rights—began filing cases seeking repeal of abortion laws. The ACLU and the James Madison Constitutional Law Institute filed suit in 1970 on behalf of the YWCA of Princeton, New Jersey, a group of doctors, and several other organizations against the state of New Jersey. The suit claimed the state's abortion law was unconstitutional because it violated the rights of women and hindered and threatened doctors. Many of these suits began making their way through the court system, as the losing side appealed the decision to the next higher court.

THree
A CASE AND A PLAINTIFF

IN TEXAS, as elsewhere, abortion rights activists had been working to ease the state's laws on abortion. Under Texas law, abortion was permitted only to save the life of the mother.

By the 1960s, an extensive underground network had developed to advise women on abortions. There was even a package deal for women to get an abortion in Mexico. For $345, a woman could get a flight to El Paso from Dallas, a motel room, hospital care, counseling, and a carnation with breakfast. Women arrived in El Paso on a Friday night, crossed the border, had an abortion on Saturday morning, and returned to Dallas by Saturday night.

In October 1969, the Women's Liberation Birth Control Information Center in Austin, Texas—an abortion referral service—placed an ad in an alternative newspaper, *The Rag*, with a hotline number for women to call. The ad attracted a big response from women eager to use the center's services. With the sudden increase in clients, however, members of the referral organization worried that their activities might come to the attention of local law enforcement officers. The members feared they would be arrested for helping Texas women get

SARAH WEDDINGTON, RIGHT, ACCEPTS A GIFT OF A SPERM WHALE, THE OFFICIAL CONNECTICUT ANIMAL, CARVED BY A WOMAN, AFTER SPEAKING AT THE 1980 CONVENTION OF THE NATIONAL FEDERATION OF DEMOCRATIC WOMEN. WEDDINGTON BECAME FAMOUS WHEN, AS A TWENTY-FOUR-YEAR-OLD LAWYER WHO HAD NEVER ARGUED A MAJOR CASE IN COURT, SHE TOOK ON *ROE* v. *WADE*. THE CASE EVENTUALLY LED TO A SUPREME COURT VICTORY FOR PRO-CHOICE ADVOCATES.

abortions. Members of the group asked a friend, Sarah Weddington, to research the law. A recent graduate of the University of Texas School of Law, Weddington had been involved in a number of women's causes. Though not a volunteer at the referral service, she quickly agreed to do the research.

At the time, Weddington was assisting one of her law professors in his work on the American Bar Association's Special Committee on the Reevaluation of Ethical Standards. The daughter of a Methodist minister, Sarah had married Ron Weddington in 1968. They lived in inexpensive student housing near the university, where Ron was attending law school. At twenty-four, she was enthusiastic, energetic, and eager to put her law skills to good use.

Weddington's research soon led her to a number of cases that related to the abortion issue. In 1965, the U.S. Supreme Court had struck down a Connecticut law that banned the use of birth control devices. In *Griswold* v. *Connecticut*, the Court ruled that married couples were protected by the right of privacy to use contraceptives. In his majority opinion, Justice William O. Douglas said the right of privacy was protected by the First, Third, Fourth, Fifth, and Ninth amendments to the Constitution. Justice John Harlan, who voted with the majority, wrote that he believed marital privacy was protected by the Fourteenth Amendment, which says that no state can deprive "any person of life, liberty, or property, without due process of law" and that no person can be denied "the equal protection of the laws."

In a separate opinion on the case, Justices Earl Warren, William J. Brennan Jr., and Arthur Goldberg wrote that the privacy right was based on the Ninth

Amendment. That amendment says that certain rights exist even if they are not named specifically in the Constitution.

Weddington thought that abortion might well be considered a private matter and that the right to privacy might apply to women seeking abortions.

"FUNDAMENTAL RIGHT"

Following the *Griswold* ruling, the California Supreme Court had voted 4 to 3 to overturn the conviction of a doctor found guilty of helping a young woman obtain an abortion. The court, in its 1969 ruling in *People* v. *Belous*, said the California law in effect at the time was unconstitutionally vague. The law allowed abortion only "to preserve the life of the woman." But it did not define the meaning of the phrase. Did it apply to a woman's threatened suicide? What if the pregnancy damaged a woman's health or shortened her life?

The ruling in *People* v. *Belous* also described abortion as a fundamental right. A fundamental right is one that is guaranteed to a person by the Constitution. To infringe on a fundamental right, a state must prove that its interests in the case far outweigh the individual's right. The judges' opinion in the *Belous* case read:

> *The fundamental right of the woman to choose whether to bear children follows from the Supreme Court's and this Court's repeated acknowledgment of a "right of privacy" and of "liberty" in matters related to marriage, family, and sex.*

In other words, the court had already acknowledged that people have the guaranteed right to make their own decisions about marriage, family, and certain sexual matters. That right, according to the judges, also covered a woman's decision whether to bear children.

Weddington knew that the Texas efforts were part of a national move to change abortion laws. And the courts—at least some of the rulings—seemed to be favorable to the abortion activists' cause.

Excited by what she had learned, Weddington shared the results of her research with the referral project's volunteers. Judy Smith, one of the organizers of the project, suggested the group go to court. She thought the organization should challenge the constitutionality of the state's abortion law. Smith and the other group members agreed that Weddington should be the one to handle the case.

The idea of handling such an important case overwhelmed Weddington. Young and inexperienced, she had never argued a contested case in court. During her fledgling law career, she had handled a few divorce cases, wills, and an adoption in court. She urged Smith to find someone with more experience.

But the group members were insistent. They had been impressed with Weddington's research. Besides, the group had little money to spend on a lawsuit, and it seemed she would work on a volunteer basis.

Weddington began to reconsider. She had never run from a challenge. As a law student, she had been one of five women in a freshman class of 125. If she took on the case, it would give her experience in constitutional law. And with their few expenses, she and her husband could manage financially on savings, her work with the professor, and Ron's part-time job.

Weddington had another reason for agreeing to take the case. In 1967, as an unmarried graduate student, she had become pregnant by Ron Weddington. The young couple, with little money and in the midst of school, decided not to have the child. They eventually found a doctor in Mexico who aborted the pregnancy. Fortunately, the doctor was skilled, and Sarah Weddington suffered no ill effects from the procedure. But the fear and uncertainty she endured left their mark. She wanted to do what she could so that others wouldn't have to go through similar experiences.

The pros outweighed the cons. Weddington agreed to take the case. At the time she agreed to fight Texas's abortion law in court, Weddington had no idea it would one day take her to the U.S. Supreme Court. She did know, however, that it would be an important and complex case and that she would need help. While a law student, Weddington had met Linda Coffee, a classmate with whom she often studied. Coffee worked for a small Dallas law firm that specialized in bankruptcy cases. Weddington asked Coffee to help with the abortion case, and Coffee agreed.

LOOKING FOR PLAINTIFFS

The first order of business for the two lawyers was to find a *plaintiff*. A plaintiff is the person on whose behalf a lawsuit is filed. A court will not hear a case based solely on an abstract question. Weddington and Coffee could not simply ask a court to decide whether the Texas abortion law was constitutional. They had to find people who were directly affected by the law and who could prove to the court that the law unjustly harmed them. Plaintiffs in such a situation are said to have *standing*.

After researching the question, the two lawyers decided against using the referral project or its volunteers

Linda Coffee does research for *Roe* v. *Wade* at her Dallas law office in 1972. Coffee worked with Sarah Weddington on the landmark case.

as plaintiffs. No one from the project had been arrested, and none of the volunteers had suffered directly from the abortion law. Without the right plaintiff, Coffee and Weddington feared, the judge might throw the case out of court before it had even had a hearing.

Weddington and Coffee spread the word among friends and associates that they were looking for a plaintiff. A woman who had heard Coffee speak about the lawsuit she was working on with Weddington said that she and her husband might be willing to be plaintiffs in the case. The woman suffered from a condition that prevented her from taking birth control pills. Her doctor had told her a pregnancy might harm her health. She and her husband used another form of birth control, but it was less reliable than birth control pills. If she were to become pregnant, an abortion seemed the only way to ensure her health. But the Texas law allowed abortions only if pregnancy endangered the mother's life. Nothing was said about the mother's *health*. The woman and her husband believed that the state law put her health at risk and was therefore unconstitutional.

Coffee and Weddington decided to accept the woman's offer. They believed she and her husband could show that the law affected them directly. Because the couple did not want their names to be used in the case, Coffee and Weddington called them John and Mary Doe in the lawsuit.

The two lawyers continued to look for another plaintiff. Lawyers often name more than one plaintiff to make sure their case is heard. That way, if one plaintiff lacks standing, the court may still hear the case of the second plaintiff. Their "ideal" plaintiff, Weddington and Coffee knew, would be a pregnant woman who wanted an abortion. Though the abortion referral project came in contact with many women who fit that description, involving them in the court case would have meant a long delay. That might have made an abortion risky or impossible. The women who sought help from the referral project wanted to undergo abortions while still in the early stages of their pregnancies.

A few weeks later, Coffee got a call from a young

woman who had been referred by a lawyer she knew, Henry McCluskey. The woman was pregnant and wanted an abortion. Her name was Norma McCorvey.

Single and in her early twenties, McCorvey said she would lose her job as a waitress if she continued her pregnancy. She had little money and had already had one child, cared for by her mother. The young woman said she could not afford to pay for an out-of-state abortion. She also said that she had been raped. In response to the lawyers' questions, she acknowledged that she had never reported the rape, and she provided few details on how she became pregnant. The lawyers decided not to claim that McCorvey had been raped if she agreed to go to court. They believed all women should be able to choose whether to have an abortion, not just rape victims. Years later, McCorvey changed her story and said she had not been raped. She said she thought the story would help her to get an abortion.

Weddington and Coffee explained the Texas law to McCorvey and outlined why they wanted to challenge it in court. They told her what role she would play in the case if she agreed to be a plaintiff. McCorvey would have to sign an affidavit stating that she was pregnant and wanted an abortion. She would not have to appear in court or answer questions from other lawyers. She would not have to pay anything to pursue the case in court. The two lawyers would handle the case for free, and others would pay court costs. And, Weddington and Coffee said, McCorvey wouldn't have to tell anyone she was the plaintiff in the case. They would use another name, or pseudonym, when they referred to her in court.

Agreeing to the terms, McCorvey signed the affidavit. From then on, the lawyers would refer to her as Jane Roe. Under that name, she would become one of the most famous plaintiffs in U.S. history.

Sarah Weddington and Linda Coffee first filed *Roe* v. *Wade* against Dallas County District Attorney Henry Wade. He made headlines when he won Jack Ruby's conviction for the murder of Lee Harvey Oswald, President John F. Kennedy's assassin, in 1963.

four
FILING SUIT

NOW THAT THEY HAD THEIR PLAINTIFFS, Weddington and Coffee had to decide where to file their suits. Most cases begin in state court. However, cases may be filed in federal court when a constitutional question, a federal law, or a treaty is at issue. A constitutional question involves rights or privileges guaranteed under the U.S. Constitution.

The lawyers were challenging a state law on constitutional issues, claiming that the law interfered with a woman's fundamental right to control her body. Because they believed the case qualified for federal review, they decided to file it in federal district court. Weddington and Coffee believed, too, that the federal courts were more liberal than the state courts. They hoped that a favorable verdict by a federal court would have an impact on other abortion laws nationwide.

The cases would be filed against Henry Wade, district attorney (DA) of Dallas County. As DA, Wade was elected to enforce the laws of the state, including the abortion law. He had gained a measure of fame as the DA who won Jack Ruby's conviction for the 1963 murder of Lee Harvey Oswald, the accused assassin of President John F. Kennedy.

On March 3, 1970, Linda Coffee filed two cases in the federal courthouse in Dallas. Once docketed (recorded on the court's schedule), the cases would become *Roe* v. *Wade* and *Doe* v. *Wade*.

The two lawyers worked hard to complete their briefs before the court deadline. Lawyers are required to state the arguments supporting their case in papers, or briefs, filed with the court. Weddington and Coffee also decided to file their cases as class-action suits. That means that the plaintiff is joined in the suit by other people in similar circumstances. In the case of *Roe*, Weddington and Coffee would argue on behalf of all pregnant women in Texas who were seeking or would seek to have an abortion and whose lives were not endangered by their pregnancies.

As Coffee and Weddington had hoped, the two cases—because they were so similar—would be heard together as companion cases. Three federal judges would hear the case: Federal District Judge William M. Taylor, Federal Circuit Judge Irving L. Goldberg, and Federal District Judge Sarah T. Hughes.

Weddington and Coffee were elated. After graduation, Coffee had been a clerk in Judge Hughes's office. The judge had made national news when she administered the oath of office to Lyndon B. Johnson aboard *Air Force One* after John F. Kennedy's assassination. Coffee viewed the judge as fair-minded and thought she might be more open to the abortion case than some other judges.

Federal court hearing

On May 22, 1970, Coffee and Weddington made their way to the Dallas Federal Courthouse for the hearing.

THROUGH THE COURT SYSTEM

First Stop: State Court

These courts go by various names, depending on the state in which they operate: circuit, district, municipal, county, or superior courts. The case is tried and decided by a judge, a panel of judges, or a jury.

The side that loses can then appeal to the next level.

First Stop: Federal Court

U.S. DISTRICT COURT—About 5 percent of cases begin their journey in federal court. Most of these cases concern federal laws, the U.S. Constitution, or disputes that involve two or more states. They are heard in one of the ninety-four U.S. district courts in the nation.

U.S. COURT OF INTERNATIONAL TRADE—Federal court cases involving international trade appear in the U.S. Court of International Trade.

U.S. CLAIMS COURT—The U.S. Claims Court hears federal cases that involve more than ten thousand dollars, American Indian claims, and some disputes with government contractors.

The loser in federal court can appeal to the next level.

Appeals: State Cases

Forty states have appeals courts that hear cases which have come from the state courts. In states without an appeals court, the case goes directly to the state supreme court.

Appeals: Federal Cases

U.S. CIRCUIT COURT—Cases appealed from U.S. District Courts go to U.S. Circuit courts of appeals. There are twelve circuit courts that handle cases from all over the nation. Each district court and every state and territory is assigned to one of the twelve circuits. Appeals in a few state cases—those that deal with rights guaranteed by the U.S. Constitution—are also heard in this court.

U.S. COURT OF APPEALS—Cases appealed from the U.S. Court of International Trade and the U.S. Claims Court are heard by the U.S. Court of Appeals for the Federal Circuit. Among the cases heard in this court are those involving patents and minor claims against the federal government.

Further Appeals: State Supreme Court

Cases appealed from state appeals courts go to the highest courts in the state—usually called supreme court. In New York, the state's highest court is called the court of appeals. Most state cases do not go beyond this point.

Final Appeals: U.S. Supreme Court

The Supreme Court is the highest court in the country. Its decision on a case is the final word. The Court decides issues that can affect every person in the nation. It has decided cases on slavery, abortion, school segregation, and many other important issues.

The Court selects the cases it will hear—usually around one hundred each year. Four of the nine justices must vote to consider a case in order for it to be heard. Almost all cases have been appealed from the lower courts (either state or federal).

Most people seeking a decision from the Court submit a petition for *certiorari*. Certiorari means that the case will be moved from a lower court to a higher court for review. The Court receives about seven thousand of these requests annually. The petition outlines the case and gives reasons why the Court should review it.

In rare cases, for example, *New York Times* v. *United States*, an issue must be decided immediately. When such a case is of national importance, the Court allows it to bypass the usual lower court system and hears the case directly.

To win a spot on the Court's docket, a case must fall within one of the following categories:

· Disputes between states and the federal government or between two or more states. It also reviews cases involving ambassadors, consuls, and foreign ministers.

· Appeals from a state court that has ruled on a federal question.

· Appeals from federal appeals courts (about two-thirds of all requests fall into this category).

Outside, demonstrators showed their support for the lawyers' case with signs that read: MY BODY, MY DECISION, and COMPULSORY PREGNANCY IS A CRUEL AND UNUSUAL PUNISHMENT. Virginia Whitehill, a Planned Parenthood volunteer and women's rights activist, had arranged the demonstration. She and other members of the committee sat in the courtroom waiting for the hearing to begin. Every seat was filled.

Before the hearing, Weddington and Coffee had agreed to join forces with two attorneys representing Dr. James H. Hallford. Dr. Hallford had been indicted and charged with performing illegal abortions in Texas. In defending their client, Dr. Hallford's attorneys, Fred Bruner and Roy L. Merrill Jr., challenged the legality of the Texas abortion law.

Standing before the three judges in the courtroom, Linda Coffee spoke first. Coffee had argued cases in court before, but most involved bankruptcy. This was the most important case the young lawyer had ever handled. Nevertheless, she set forth the technicalities of the case in her usual calm style.

First, she defended the plaintiffs' right to a hearing. They had standing and were entitled to sue in federal court, she argued, because the Texas law affected them directly and interfered with their constitutional rights. She contended that the law violated the First, Fourth, Fifth, Eighth, Ninth, and Fourteenth amendments. Coffee then discussed how the Texas law violated the First Amendment. She said the ban on abortions interfered with the right of doctors to talk to their clients about a medical procedure.

The judges didn't appear to be impressed by the argument. Judge Hughes asked her to comment on how the Ninth Amendment applied to the case. The Ninth Amendment says the people retain certain rights even though they are not specifically noted in the Constitution.

Coffee replied, "I don't think it makes any difference . . . whether you say that the rights involved are First Amendment rights or Ninth Amendment rights. I feel they are so important that they deserve the special protection that has been accorded to First Amendment rights."

Coffee made a few other points, and then her time was up. Weddington took her place before the judges. She was twenty-five years old and had never before argued a contested case in court. Her voice shook as she began her statement, but she soon gained confidence. In a clear, strong voice, softened by her soft Texas drawl, Weddington began to state the facts of her case.

She noted that the state clung to the law in order to protect what it said were the rights of the fetus. But, she questioned, does the fetus have rights if it is not human? And how do we know, she asked, when a fetus becomes human? "It is almost impossible to define a point at which life begins," Weddington told the court.

Judge Goldberg asked her to talk about how the Texas law might violate the Ninth Amendment. Did the state have a "compelling reason," Goldberg asked, to override the right to an abortion?

The only compelling reason for the state to regulate abortion, Weddington replied, was to protect the woman. As long as abortions were performed by licensed doctors, she argued, the state had no good reason to ban the procedure. And, she noted, there was also no reason for the state to set up different standards for married and single women. Once again, the court signalled that time was up.

During their allotted time, Dr. James H. Hallford's attorneys, Bruner and Merrill, argued that the Texas abortion law was unconstitutionally vague. At the signal, they sat down. The plaintiffs' part of the hearing was over.

Federal Circuit Judge Irving L. Goldberg. Goldberg served on the three-judge panel that heard the *Roe* and *Doe* cases in federal court in Dallas in May 1970. In June the court ruled that the Texas abortion ban was unconstitutional, but the panel did not order the state to stop enforcing the law. As a result, the cases progressed to the Supreme Court.

Arguing the State's Case

For the next thirty minutes, Jay Floyd and John Tolle argued the state's case. Neatly dressed and professional-looking, Floyd worked as a lawyer in the enforcement division of the Texas attorney general's office. He specialized in liquor law.

Floyd argued that the plaintiffs had no right to sue in federal court. He noted that the state had never prosecuted a woman for undergoing an abortion. He said women could not say that the law hurt them. Therefore, he argued, Jane Roe and Mary Doe had no standing. Jane Roe, he noted, had probably already had her baby by now. Even if she were still pregnant, he noted, it was too late for her to undergo a safe abortion. Mary Doe, he continued, was not pregnant and never had been.

The judges did not appear to be convinced by Floyd's statements. Judge Goldberg countered by saying that some of the children involved in the school desegregation cases of the 1950s had long since graduated from high school by the time the court heard their cases.

"What would give them [Roe and Doe] standing in a case like this to test the constitutionality of this statute?" Judge Hughes asked Floyd. "Apparently you don't think that anybody has standing."

Floyd went on to argue that the Constitution does not mention a "right" to abortion. He disputed Coffee's claim that the First Amendment protected abortion. Judge Hughes told him the court agreed with his view of the First Amendment in this case.

The judges then questioned Floyd about the Ninth Amendment and issues of vagueness. Instead of arguing directly, he went to the heart of the state's case. Texas, he asserted, had to protect the fetus. That was the state's "compelling interest" in limiting abortions. He argued further that the right to privacy cited in other cases means only the right to be left alone. It had nothing to do with abortion, Floyd contended.

John Tolle, a lawyer with the Dallas DA's office, took over for Floyd. Although he accepted the fact that no one knew when life began, he argued that the state still had "a right to protect life . . . in whatever stage it may be in."

FEDERAL DISTRICT JUDGE SARAH T. HUGHES. HUGHES WAS ALSO A MEMBER OF THE THREE-JUDGE PANEL THAT INITIALLY RULED THE TEXAS ABORTION LAW UNCONSTITUTIONAL. IN 1963, HUGHES HAD WON NATIONAL RECOGNITION AS THE JUDGE WHO SWORE IN LYNDON B. JOHNSON AS PRESIDENT AFTER JOHN F. KENNEDY'S ASSASSINATION.

He contended that it was up to the state legislature to decide when abortions should be allowed. Tolle finished by saying that the state put the fetus's right to life ahead of the woman's right to privacy. The arguments ended. All either side could do now was wait for the judges to rule on the cases.

On June 17, 1970, the court handed down its thirteen-page decision. The Texas abortion law, all three judges said, was unconstitutional. They ruled that abortion was a fundamental right, and the law unconstitutionally interfered with that right. Women, the judges said, had a right to choose not to have children. That right, they said, was based on the Ninth Amendment.

The ruling supported Dr. Hallford's claim also, that the law was too vague. According to the court, the Fourteenth Amendment's "due process of law" clause protected Dr. Hallford from being punished by a law that was unclear. The judges also ruled that Jane Roe and Dr. Hallford had a right to sue but that the Does did not because they lacked standing.

For Norma McCorvey, the Jane Roe in the case, the decision came too late. Shortly after the court ruling, she had her baby and put her up for adoption.

Weddington and Coffee's victory celebration was short-lived. The court had ruled in their favor that the law was unconstitutional. But the judges had not ordered the state to stop enforcing the law. The court, it appeared, did not want to interfere further with state government. Henry Wade, the Dallas DA, announced publicly that he would continue to enforce the old law. "Apparently, we're still free to try them [doctors who performed abortions not allowed by the old law], so we'll do just that," he told the press shortly after the decision was announced. Despite the court decision, a woman still could not obtain a legal abortion in Texas unless her life was at risk.

on to the supreme court

Coffee and Weddington decided to appeal. Since the judges had not issued an order to enforce the law, the plaintiffs had a right to take the matter to a higher court. Usually, lawyers appealing cases work their way through successively higher levels in the court system. Normally, a federal case would be appealed to the circuit court. Only after that would it be appealed to the U.S. Supreme Court.

But the state had made it clear it would continue to enforce a law that had been ruled unconstitutional. Because of that, Weddington and Coffee were permitted to skip a step. They appealed directly to the Supreme Court.

Each year the Supreme Court receives thousands of requests to hear cases. These requests are called petitions for certiorari. Most of the petitions are rejected outright. Some are ruled improper. Others don't qualify to be heard by the Supreme Court for other reasons. The remaining petitions are reviewed by the Supreme Court justices. Four justices must vote to hear a case if the full Court is to consider it. At the time the *Roe* case was argued, in the early 1970s, the Supreme Court heard arguments on only 100 to 150 cases a year.

Cases involving abortion were pending in eleven states in 1970. Three-judge federal courts were considering another twenty cases on the subject. Lawyers in five abortion cases, including *Roe*, had petitioned the Supreme Court for review that year.

On May 21, 1971, the Supreme Court published the

list of cases it would hear during the coming October term. *Roe* v. *Wade*, number 808 on the Court docket, and *Doe* v. *Bolton*, a Georgia abortion case, number 971 on the docket, were among those to be heard by the Court during its next session. The *Roe* brief, written arguments supporting the lawyers' case, would be due June 17. The state would have to submit its brief thirty days later. After the justices had reviewed the briefs, they would schedule oral arguments. At that time, lawyers for both sides would present their case in person before the Supreme Court.

Weddington and Coffee had a mountain of work to do before then.

Harriet Pilpel, the lead attorney with Planned Parenthood Federation of America, advised Coffee and Weddington on the *Roe* and *Doe* cases. She had worked on and helped win *Griswold* v. *Connecticut*, which overturned the ban on birth control devices.

FIVE
MAKING A CASE FOR ABORTION

THE TEXAS CASE HAD DRAWN THE ATTENTION of abortion rights activists nationwide. Harriet Pilpel, the lead attorney with Planned Parenthood Federation of America, telephoned with advice. Pilpel had worked on the *Griswold* case, winning a ruling from the Supreme Court that married couples were protected by the right of privacy to use contraceptives.

The case would require a great deal of research, and both Coffee and Weddington had full-time jobs. They had volunteered to work on the case for free, but they needed money to pay court fees and to print the thick stack of papers supporting their case. Hundreds of pages had to be printed for the Court and photocopied for the opposing lawyers.

Roy Lucas, who had worked on the *Vuitch* appeal to the Supreme Court, offered his help. Milan Vuitch, the doctor arrested by District of Columbia police for performing illegal abortions, had won a ruling in federal court that the district's abortion law was unconstitutionally vague, but the Supreme Court later upheld the law. As director and general counsel of the James Madison Constitutional Law Institute in New York, Lucas was deeply involved in the abortion issue. He offered the Institute staff's help in researching the briefs for the Supreme Court and said he would pay some of the costs. Coffee and Weddington accepted Lucas's offer.

Weddington had begun work as assistant city attorney in Fort Worth, Texas, in the fall of 1970. She was the first woman to hold the job. Once word got out that the *Roe* case was headed for the Supreme Court, Weddington's boss gave her a choice. She could continue to work for the city, or she could quit and work on the case. Weddington decided she couldn't pass up the chance to argue a case as important as *Roe* before the Supreme Court. She quit her job to work on the case full-time. She and Ron also decided to move back to Austin and set up their own law practice there.

With the June 17 deadline looming, Lucas had asked the Court for a postponement. The Court had set the new deadline for August 1. Weddington headed for New York, where she would work part-time for the Institute and use the resources there to work on the *Roe* case. Leaving Ron to run the couple's newly established law firm, she arrived in New York in mid-June. Lucas arranged for her to stay in a small room at the Women's Medical Center in Manhattan.

preparing the case

During the long, hot summer days, Weddington worked with the Institute staff researching and writing briefs for a stack of abortion cases. But this left little time to devote to the *Roe* case. As the summer wore on, Weddington realized she would never be able to finish the *Roe* brief by August 1. Again, the Supreme Court granted an extension—this time to August 17.

To meet the deadline, Weddington knew she would

have to get additional help. Linda Coffee was working full-time with the bankruptcy firm in Dallas. The Institute staff was swamped with work. Weddington called her husband, Ron, who agreed to come to New York to help with the *Roe* brief.

For the next five weeks, the two young lawyers reviewed every abortion case and decision they could find. They studied other Supreme Court decisions that might relate to their case. They used these past decisions, called *precedents*, to bolster their arguments in the *Roe* brief.

Ron worked on the technical parts of the argument. Sarah focused on the merits of the case, the reasons why she believed the Court should decide in Roe's favor. Students at the Institute pitched in. One helped with the research. Another proofread the brief.

At the time, the Supreme Court limited the length of briefs to 150 pages. On those pages, the *Roe* lawyers had to list all their reasons for claiming that the Texas abortion law was unconstitutional. They argued that the abortion law violated their plaintiffs' rights guaranteed by the First, Fourth, Ninth, and Fourteenth amendments. Citing experts in several fields, the brief outlined the history of abortion law in the United States. It detailed the medical, legal, and religious aspects of abortion. The brief also described how pregnancy affected women's lives and mental health.

Abortion rights groups and others filed briefs that would also be submitted to the Supreme Court regarding the case. Lawyers whose clients could be affected by the *Roe* decision filed these arguments, called *amicus curiae* ("friend of the court") briefs. Each brief addressed one aspect of the *Roe* argument.

Jimmye Kimmey, executive director of the Association for the Study of Abortion, volunteered to organize the *amicus* briefs. Her association provided information on abortion to other organizations. Religious groups, Planned Parenthood Federation of America, the American Association of Planned Parenthood Physicians, Zero Population Growth, medical groups, law professors, and women's organizations all submitted briefs. A total of forty-two *amicus* briefs were filed in support of *Roe*.

Among the groups filing *amicus* briefs on the state's side were the National Right to Life Committee, Women for the Unborn, and the Association of Texas Diocesan Attorneys. The attorneys general in Arizona, Connecticut, Kentucky, Nebraska, and Utah also filed a brief supporting Texas. When stacked together the briefs for both sides stood a foot tall.

The paper mound continued to grow—as did the bill for expenses that the *Roe* lawyers faced. In addition to the lengthy brief, the *Roe* documents contained a five-hundred-page appendix with tables, graphs, statistics, articles, and other information related to abortion. Ruth Bowers, a Texas philanthropist who donated generously to Planned Parenthood, footed much of the bill for printing the *Roe* brief and other expenses mounting in the suit. The James Madison Constitutional Law Institute picked up some of the court filing costs and provided research assistance as well as the free room for Ron and Sarah. Other funds came from abortion rights supporters nationwide, who sent in donations. Among them was Thomas Cabot, a Boston businessman, who gave $15,000 to the cause. A smaller gift came from a doctor in Harlem who wrote about the horror of seeing women suffer from illegal abortions. Medical school professors, doctors, lawyers, law students, members of women's groups, and others volunteered to help with research and other tasks needed to finish the brief.

While Weddington and others were immersed in the paperwork involving the case, the plaintiff was far removed from the activity. Norma McCorvey, after giving birth, had disappeared from the scene. She had not attended the federal court hearing because of her pregnancy, and, later, she would not be at the Supreme Court hearings.

WEDDINGTON FOR THE PLAINTIFF

On August 17, the *Roe* lawyers delivered forty copies of their brief to the U.S. Supreme Court—just in time for the deadline. During the weeks that followed, they would spend all their time preparing for oral arguments before the Court.

Lucas had listed himself as lead attorney when he filed the Court documents for *Roe*. He reasoned that he had more court experience than Weddington. But Weddington, who had been involved in the effort from the start, wanted the chance to argue the landmark case. Many of those who had worked on the case with Weddington agreed that a woman should argue before the Court. They urged Weddington to accept the challenge. On November 24, Linda Coffee sent a notice to the Supreme Court listing Weddington as the lawyer presenting oral arguments for *Roe*. She noted that Jane Roe and Mary and John Doe, the plaintiffs, had requested Weddington. The court clerk recorded Weddington as the lawyer who would argue for *Roe*. Jay Floyd would present the case for the state of Texas.

NORMA MCCORVEY, THE "ROE" IN *ROE V. WADE*, HAD A CHANGE OF HEART IN THE MID-1990S AND BECAME A SPOKESWOMAN FOR THE ANTIABORTION FORCES. IN JUNE 2003, SHE FILED A SUIT ASKING THE GOVERNMENT TO REVERSE THE CASE THAT MADE HER FAMOUS.

Norma McCorvey:
FROM ABORTION RIGHTS SYMBOL TO PRO-LIFE ACTIVIST

Much has changed in Norma McCorvey's life since she first became Jane Roe and the symbol for abortion rights. Back then, in 1969, she was a tough, twenty-one-year-old carnival worker down on her luck. Married at sixteen, McCorvey had her first child before she turned eighteen. Her mother took custody of the little girl after McCorvey divorced. She had a second daughter after becoming involved with a man she decided she did not want to marry. The father of the little girl took over the child's care.

Pregnant a third time by another man, she went to an illegal abortion clinic in Dallas, but the place had been closed down by the police. Her doctor suggested she talk to a local attorney about putting the baby up for adoption. The lawyer referred her to two young Dallas lawyers, Linda Coffee and Sarah Weddington.

McCorvey, still hoping she could get an abortion, agreed to be the plaintiff the two lawyers needed to make their case. She knew she did not want a baby, could not support a child, and could not get a regular job because she was pregnant. "I agreed to be the plaintiff," she later said, "because I was [angry]. I thought . . . maybe, if I stuck with these two people, they could really do it. And sure enough, they did, but not for me, no."

Long before the case ever made it to the Supreme Court, McCorvey gave birth to another daughter, who was adopted. Depressed, the young woman tried to commit suicide. Eventually, she got a job and began to turn her life around.

For many years the *Roe* case had little impact on her life. Because the lawyers had used the name Jane Roe in the suit, most people did not know McCorvey's connection to the case. She herself had never had an abortion. "I really felt like I had been cheated because the decision didn't help me," she said.

With the encouragement of friends, she decided, in 1980, to reveal to the press that she was Jane Roe. She said she finally realized that she had "helped to change the course of history for all the women in America." The revelation marked another turning point in her life.

For the next several years she took part in pro-choice rallies once a year on the anniversary of the *Roe* decision but did little else to support the cause. That changed after someone shot up her house in the early morning hours of April 4, 1989. "The shooting made me determined to be more public," she wrote in an article published in 1991. Soon after the incident, she became the poster girl for the pro-choice movement. She carried protest signs at rallies, promoted the pro-choice position during interviews with the press, and worked at an abortion clinic. "This issue is the only thing I live for. I live, eat, breathe, think everything about abortion," she told a reporter.

Then, in 1995, her life took another unexpected turn. Members of Operation Rescue, an aggressive pro-life group, opened an office next door to the abortion clinic where McCorvey worked. As a blue-collar worker with little education, McCorvey had never felt completely accepted by the women who led the pro-choice movement. She had had a falling out with Weddington and had not been invited to participate in the White House celebration of the twentieth anniversary of *Roe*.

At first she clashed with the Operation Rescue protesters who picketed outside the clinic where she worked. But eventually, McCorvey came to admire them. Several of the protesters became her friends, and in 1995 a minister working with Operation Rescue baptized McCorvey. Announcing her conversion to the world, she said she had joined Operation Rescue and was working for the pro-life cause. "The poster child for abortion just jumped off the poster and into the arms of Jesus Christ," a pro-life supporter remarked.

In 1997 McCorvey broke her ties with Operation Rescue after a bitter eleven-day protest in San Diego. Today she runs her own nonprofit group, Roe No More Ministry, dedicated to the pro-life cause. In June 2003 McCorvey filed suit seeking to overturn *Roe* v. *Wade*. The suit was dismissed because it had been filed too long after the original judgment had been issued. Nevertheless, McCorvey remains committed to the pro-life cause.

"I'm one hundred percent pro-life," she writes on her Web site. "No exceptions. No compromise."

From left, Ron Weddington, Sarah Weddington, U.S. Representative George Mahon, and Sarah's mother, Lena Katherine Ragle, pose for a picture in Washington, D.C., on December 13, 1971, the day the Supreme Court heard the first arguments in the *Roe* v. *Wade* case.

Few cases are won in oral arguments, according to court experts. But, the experts agree, some cases are lost because they were poorly argued. Weddington wanted to make sure she was well-prepared. The lawyers were to argue their cases in the Supreme Court on December 13, 1971. Weddington immersed herself in the case. She attended a Supreme Court hearing and watched the proceedings carefully. Preparing for her own appearance, she noted where each lawyer stood, what they wore, how the Court operated.

She also wrote notes on index cards and organized them for easy reference. Each card had a topic written in big letters, with more information in smaller print. Weddington taped the cards inside a manila folder that she would hold while arguing her case before the Supreme Court.

She rehearsed her performance in two moot courts. The moot, or pretend, courts were set up like the Supreme Court, with volunteers playing the roles of the justices. Weddington went through her arguments just as if the court were the real thing. The pretend justices interrupted her arguments with questions. In real Supreme Court proceedings, justices often ask questions of the lawyers as they present their cases.

During their research for the brief, she and Ron had studied the decisions issued by each justice. They had read about the justices' politics, their interests, and their personal lives. Now Weddington reviewed that information, trying to tailor her arguments to each justice.

Warren E. Burger, chief justice of the Court, and Harry A. Blackmun had often been called the "Minnesota Twins." Both were from that state and had gone to Sunday school together as children. Both had been appointed by President Richard Nixon, Burger in 1969 and Blackmun in 1970. Blackmun had voted with Burger on almost every case during his first term. Court watchers put both Nixon justices in the conservative wing of the Court. They were likely to support strict abortion laws.

William O. Douglas had been appointed in 1939 by President Franklin D. Roosevelt. The oldest and most senior member, Douglas was considered the Court's most liberal justice. He most certainly would vote to strike down the abortion laws.

Joining Douglas in the liberal wing were William J. Brennan Jr. and Thurgood Marshall. Brennan, appointed by President Dwight D. Eisenhower in 1956, had voted to strike down the law banning birth control devices in *Griswold* v. *Connecticut*. He would probably vote for *Roe*. Marshall, the first and only black member then on the Court, would also be likely to vote against conservative abortion laws. Appointed by President Lyndon B. Johnson in 1967, Marshall was a strong supporter of civil and individual rights.

That left Byron R. White and Potter Stewart. Stewart, appointed in 1958 by President Eisenhower, had voted against most of the liberal opinions of the Warren Court. He had also voted against *Griswold*. But other votes had placed him in the middle of the Court. White, likewise, tended toward the middle with his votes. Appointed by President John F. Kennedy in 1962, White had cast his vote for the right of privacy in the *Griswold* case. But he was also "tough" on crime and voted with Burger on those issues.

Two other justices, John Marshall Harlan and Hugo Black Jr., had resigned in September due to ill health. Nixon had appointed Lewis F. Powell Jr. and William H. Rehnquist to the Court. Because they had not yet been sworn in, they would not hear the case. The case would be heard by a seven-member Court.

Weddington would have thirty minutes to present her arguments. She would be followed by the state's attorney, who would argue his case for thirty minutes, also. During the same hearing, the Court would also hear arguments in the Georgia abortion case, *Doe* v. *Bolton*. The plaintiffs in that case claimed the more liberal Georgia abortion law was unconstitutional. Georgia allowed abortions but required the woman to get permission from a panel of doctors. The Court would review both types of laws: Texas's strict law and Georgia's more liberal one. A decision in the cases would affect abortion laws throughout the nation.

The members of the U.S. Supreme Court who ruled on the *Roe* case.
Seated, from left: Potter Stewart, William O. Douglas, Chief Justice
Warren E. Burger, William J. Brennan Jr., and Byron R. White.
Standing, from left: Lewis F. Powell Jr., Thurgood Marshall, Harry
A. Blackmun, and William H. Rehnquist.

SIX
SUPREME COURT ARGUMENTS

"THE HONORABLE, THE CHIEF JUSTICE, *and the associate justices of the Supreme Court of the United States! Oyez, oyez, oyez! All persons having business before the Honorable, the Supreme Court of the United States, are admonished to draw near and give their attention, for the Court is now sitting. God save the United States and this Honorable Court."*

With those words the clerk announced the opening of the Supreme Court's session on December 13, 1971. Arguments on the two abortion cases were scheduled that morning. The seven justices stepped from behind velvet curtains and took their seats at the bench. Chief Justice Burger sat in the center, with Douglas on his right and Brennan on his left. The associate justices sat in order of how long they had served on the Court. Blackmun, the newest justice, sat to the far left of Burger. Next to him was White. To the far right of the chief justice sat Marshall, the second-newest associate justice. Next to Blackmun sat White. Stewart sat next to Marshall.

"LADIES' DAY"
The Court staff referred to the proceedings as "Ladies' Day." Three women would be presenting cases.

Weddington would argue for *Roe*, Margie Pitts Hames would argue for *Doe*, and Dorothy Beasley would plead for the state of Georgia in the *Doe* case. Few women attended law school then, and even fewer appeared before the Supreme Court to argue cases. That fact became apparent to the women in the abortion cases when they discovered the lawyers' lounge contained no women's restroom.

Weddington would be the first to speak to the justices. The lawyers sat in an area directly in front of the bench. This area was divided into two sides by a central corridor. Weddington's table was on the left. Sitting with her were Linda Coffee and Roy Lucas. Ron Weddington sat in the lawyers' section. Behind Weddington's table, Margie Pitts Hames and the other attorney for *Doe* in the Georgia case sat waiting for their turn to speak. At the front table to the right, Jay Floyd and Texas Attorney General Crawford Martin conferred with their team representing Texas in the *Roe* case. Behind them sat Dorothy Beasley and the rest of the team for Georgia.

Weddington's mother and a crowd of supporters from Texas and elsewhere who had been active in the fight to legalize abortion took their seats in the audience. The couple known as John and Mary Doe in the federal court suit sat in seats reserved for them by Weddington. Norma McCorvey did not attend. About 350 people filled the small room. Members of the press occupied all eighty-five seats reserved for them.

Everyone rose as the justices walked in and took their seats. In hushed silence, the audience sat down. At 10:07 a.m., Chief Justice Burger addressed Weddington. "Mrs. Weddington, you may proceed whenever you are ready."

Facing the Justices

The young lawyer rose and stepped to the lectern before the bench. It was only the second time she had appeared in court in a contested case.

Weddington spoke of the effect of pregnancy on a woman's life. She noted that the decision to have children is a fundamental right and should be made by the woman. "Because of the impact on the woman," Weddington told the Court, "this certainly . . . is a matter . . . of such fundamental and basic concern to the woman involved that she should be allowed to make the choice as to whether to continue or terminate her pregnancy."

White asked her what part of the Constitution guaranteed a right to abortion. In its majority opinion, the Court had already ruled in the *Griswold* case that the right to privacy is based on the Ninth Amendment. Weddington said the Ninth Amendment could also apply to abortions. In addition, she said, the right to an abortion could be found in the Fourteenth Amendment. The due process clause of the Fourteenth Amendment had been used as a basis of Judge John Harlan's opinion in the *Griswold* case.

"I do feel that the Ninth Amendment is an appropriate place for the freedom to rest," Weddington told White. "I think the Fourteenth Amendment is an equally appropriate place, under the rights of persons to life [and] liberty. . . . In as far as liberty is meaningful, that liberty to these women would mean liberty from being forced to continue the unwanted pregnancy."

In response to further questioning from White, Weddington said, "We originally brought the suit alleging . . . the due process clause, [the] equal protection clause, the Ninth Amendment, and a variety of others."

"And anything else that might have been appropriate," added White.

The audience and Weddington laughed. White made it sound like the plaintiffs were using everything—including the kitchen sink—to win their case.

The justices continued their questions. In answering, Weddington made the point that the state of Texas and the Constitution granted rights to people only after birth. The fetus had no rights in law. Asked if Texas law gave rights to unborn children regarding trusts and wills, she answered, "No, your honor, only if they are born alive."

After a few more questions, the red light on the lectern lit up. That was the signal that Weddington's time was over. She had spoken for twenty-five minutes. Her final five minutes would be used later to argue points the state's attorney made. "Thank you, Mrs. Weddington," Burger said. She sat down, and Jay Floyd stepped up to make his case.

"It's an old joke," Floyd began, "but when a man argues against two beautiful ladies like this, they're going to have the last word." His attempt at humor failed. No one laughed.

Floyd continued by saying that Jane Roe had no right to plead her case in Court because she was no longer pregnant. Justice Stewart noted that the case was a class action, representing many women. Then Stewart remarked that "there are, at any given time, unmarried, pregnant females in the state of Texas." That comment drew laughter from the audience.

Floyd persisted in saying that there was no way a pregnant woman could get a Supreme Court hearing because by the time a woman's case got to that Court, she would no longer be pregnant. "There are situations in which no remedy is provided," he noted. "I think [a woman] makes her choice prior to the time she becomes pregnant. That is the time of choice."

"Maybe she makes her choice when she decides to live in Texas," came Stewart's response. Once again, the audience laughed.

Stewart asked Floyd to explain what interest the state had in the abortion question. He replied that the state's primary interest was to protect the life of the fetus. "There is life from the moment of impregnation," he said.

Marshall asked if he had scientific data to prove his statement. Floyd noted that he had outlined the development of the fetus "from about seven to nine days after conception."

"Well, what about six days?" asked Marshall. "[T]his statute goes all the way back to one hour."

Floyd stuttered out an answer. "I don't—Mr. Justice, it—there are unanswerable questions in this field, I—" Laughter from the audience ended his comments, as Marshall said, "I appreciate it, I appreciate it."

Weddington gave a short rebuttal, and the arguments in *Roe* v. *Wade* ended.

After a brief break, the attorneys in the Georgia case presented their arguments. Hames argued that the state's abortion law, with all its requirements, was unconstitutional. The restrictions in the law made it too difficult for women to obtain abortions, she said. A woman seeking an abortion in Georgia had to get permission from two doctors and a hospital panel. The state's attorneys argued that it was the state's right to regulate abortion.

The red light on the lectern lit up for the fourth time that day. The abortion issue was now in the hands of the Supreme Court justices.

DECISION POSTPONED

After oral arguments, the justices meet to discuss cases. They are the only ones allowed to attend the meeting. The justices review the points made in court and in the briefs, and discuss precedents that relate to the case and then vote on the case.

If the chief justice votes with the majority, he may assign one of the justices who also voted with the majority to write the opinion. Sometimes the chief justice writes the opinion himself. The opinion outlines the reasons behind the Court's decision in a case. If the chief justice votes with the minority, then the associate justice with the most seniority who is in the majority assigns the writing of the case.

A justice may spend several months researching and writing the opinion. During that time, other justices may write their own opinions. Those who go along with the majority but disagree with the reasons behind the vote may write concurring opinions. Those who oppose the majority vote may write dissents.

The final opinion may contain passages from a number of drafts written by several justices. To win support for the majority opinion, a justice may change the wording or include a section suggested by another justice.

Once the majority opinion has been written, the justices decide what their final positions will be on the case. Justices who agree with the opinion will join it— that is, agree to put their names on it. Others may choose to join a dissent or a separate, concurring opinion. Sometimes, the outcome of the case can change as justices who once supported the majority opinion decide, instead, to join a dissent. If a majority of the justices join the dissent, then it becomes the majority opinion.

After its final deliberations the Court announces its decision, and the majority opinion is published. It is this document that becomes the basis of law. Attorneys will use it as a precedent when pleading cases.

Deciding the abortion case was particularly difficult for the justices. They knew what an emotional issue it was. White and Burger argued that the right to regulate abortions should remain with the states. White voted to uphold the law. Burger put off voting for the moment. The three liberals—Marshall, Douglas, and Brennan—voted as expected to strike down the laws as unconstitutional.

Blackmun had been an attorney for the Mayo Clinic for ten years. He saw the issue from the doctors' viewpoint. Both he and Stewart favored lifting some restrictions against abortion that they thought hindered doctors from treating their patients. But they didn't vote to strike down the laws altogether.

Burger decided there weren't enough votes on either side to determine a majority. Instead, he asked Blackmun to write an opinion. The justices would vote on the case after the opinion was written.

Blackmun devoted himself to the job. He spent hours at the Court's library, going over medical research and reviewing law texts. The term was to end by July 4. The justices would have to have a decision on the abortion cases by then.

U.S. SUPREME COURT JUSTICE WILLIAM O. DOUGLAS TALKS TO THE PRESS IN 1970. DOUGLAS, A STRONG DEFENDER OF INDIVIDUAL RIGHTS, WAS CONSIDERED THE COURT'S MOST LIBERAL MEMBER IN 1971, WHEN *ROE* V. *WADE* WAS FIRST HEARD.

Finally, in mid-May, Blackmun showed his draft to the other justices. Stewart, Douglas, Marshall, and Brennan agreed to join Blackmun's opinion. White disagreed with the opinion and issued a dissent. After reading White's opinion, Blackmun decided he needed to rewrite his own document. He withdrew the opinion and suggested that the case be argued again in the fall. He believed the case was an important one and should be decided by the full, nine-member Court.

Douglas was angry over the delay. The two new justices, Rehnquist and Powell, were appointed by Nixon, who personally opposed abortion. Douglas assumed that the new members of the Court would vote against a right to abortion. He also believed Burger would try to pressure Blackmun into changing his vote, tipping the balance in favor of retaining the abortion laws. Douglas threatened to publish a memo severely criticizing Burger's handling of the case if the decision was delayed.

The other justices urged Douglas not to publish the memo. It would weaken the Court, they argued. Blackmun told Douglas he would not change his vote. Finally, Douglas agreed not to publish the memo. On the last day of the term, the Court announced its decision to ask for rearguments in the two abortion cases. Douglas dissented.

EDMUND S. MUSKIE TALKS TO THE PRESS IN FRONT OF THE *UNION LEADER* NEWSPAPER OFFICES IN MANCHESTER, NEW HAMPSHIRE, IN 1972 DURING HIS UNSUCCESSFUL BID TO WIN THE DEMOCRATIC NOMINATION FOR PRESIDENT. MUSKIE, A CATHOLIC, OPPOSED ABORTION.

BACK TO POLITICS

The Supreme Court's hearing of the abortion cases had focused attention on the issue. It became one of the issues discussed during the 1972 presidential campaign. Both Nixon and Edmund S. Muskie, a Catholic who was running for the Democratic nomination, took stands against abortion.

PRESIDENT RICHARD M. NIXON WAVES TO AN ENTHUSIASTIC CROWD DURING HIS SUCCESSFUL REELECTION CAMPAIGN IN 1972. HIS WIFE, PAT, SITS BESIDE HIM. NIXON TOOK A STAND AGAINST ABORTION DURING THE CAMPAIGN.

Opposition to abortion continued to grow. On April 16, 1972, a "Right to Life Sunday" attracted ten thousand protesters in New York. Pro-lifers began to make progress in their efforts to reverse state legislation that eased abortion restrictions. After the razor-thin vote that struck down New York's abortion law, the pro-life camp took aim at politicians who had supported the action. In upcoming elections, Right to Life groups—by then, well-organized and growing—helped defeat several pro-choice candidates. They also lobbied hard for their position, visiting the state house and talking with law-makers day after day.

The strategies won the pro-life activists a major victory. In May 1972, the New York State Legislature passed a bill that would have put limits on abortion in that state again. Governor Nelson Rockefeller vetoed the bill on May 13, 1972. He said, "I do not believe it is right for one group to impose its vision of morality on an entire society. . . . I can see no justification now for repealing this reform and thus condemning hundreds of thousands of women to the Dark Ages again."

Although the pro-lifers lost the battle, they gained valuable insight into how to influence legislation. They would use these lessons in future pro-life campaigns.

Roe v. *Wade*: ROUND TWO

After arguing the *Roe* case before the Supreme Court, Sarah Weddington had returned to her Texas law firm. In late spring, she won a tough primary fight against three men as Democratic candidate for the Texas House of Representatives. That November, Weddington would win the general election for the House seat.

Meanwhile, the Court had announced that the *Roe* and Georgia cases would be heard again on October 11. As the day approached, the lawyers once again headed for Washington, D.C. Ron Weddington joined Sarah and Linda Coffee at the table before the bench.

Weddington, standing this time before nine justices, was the first to speak. The arguments went much as before, but this time it seemed to observers that Weddington was better prepared. Although the right to privacy is not spelled out in the Constitution, the Court had recognized the privacy right in a number of previous cases. The right of parents to send their children to private schools, the right to determine when to have offspring, the right to choose one's spouse, the right to use birth control devices—all had been granted by the Court. And all had been based on the right to privacy, Weddington noted. The abortion right, she argued, should fall into the same category.

White asked her if she would lose her case if the Court ruled that the fetus was a person.

Weddington answered that the Court would then have to balance the rights of the mother against the rights of the fetus. But, she noted, a fetus was not treated as a person under either the Constitution or its amendments.

Listening to the tapes of the oral arguments years later, researchers commented that the state's attorneys did not seem as well-prepared. Unlike Weddington, they did not seem to have benefitted from the chance to argue the case a second time.

Robert Flowers, Texas assistant attorney general, argued the case this time for the state. He laid out his position: A fetus is a human being from conception and therefore has constitutional rights. Stewart asked if Flowers knew of any case where an unborn fetus was considered a person under the Fourteenth Amendment. Flowers had to admit he did not.

Later Blackmun asked if those in the medical profession disagreed over when life began. Flowers acknowledged that they did. He noted that the Texas law balanced the rights of the fetus and the mother. In cases where the mother's life was threatened, he said, the state chose to protect the mother. In all other cases, the state chose to protect the fetus. He also noted that the Court had protected the rights of the minority in the past.

"We say that this is a minority . . . " he told the Court. "Who is speaking for these children? Where is the counsel for these unborn children, whose life is being taken?"

Weddington used her final five minutes to rebut Flowers' statements.

She told the justices:

We are not here to advocate abortion. . . . We are here to advocate that the decision as to whether or not a particular woman will continue to carry or will terminate a pregnancy is a decision that should be made by that individual, that in fact she has a constitutional right to make that decision for herself, and that the state has shown no interest in [or sufficient legal status to allow] interfering with that decision.

Weddington sat down, and the lawyers in the Georgia case presented their arguments. The abortion issue was once again in the hands of the Court.

(Slip Opinion)

SUPREME COURT OF THE UNITED STATES

Syllabus

ROE ET AL. *v.* WADE, DISTRICT ATTORNEY OF DALLAS COUNTY

APPEAL FROM THE UNITED STATES DISTRICT COURT FOR THE NORTHERN DISTRICT OF TEXAS

No. 70–18. Argued December 13, 1971—Reargued October 11, 1972—Decided January 22, 1973

A COPY OF THE *ROE* V. *WADE* OPINION SIGNED BY THE NINE U.S. SUPREME COURT JUSTICES WHO DECIDED THE LANDMARK CASE. THE DOCUMENT WAS PROVIDED BY SARAH WEDDINGTON, THE YOUNG LAWYER WHO ARGUED ON BEHALF OF ROE.

seven
A MOMENTOUS DECISION

AT 10:00 a.m. on January 22, 1973, the U.S. Supreme Court ruled that the Texas abortion law was unconstitutional. The Court also struck down the Georgia abortion law. Burger, Blackmun, Powell, Stewart, Brennan, Douglas, and Marshall voted in the majority. Rehnquist and White opposed the decision. The highest court in the land, by a seven-to-two margin, had declared abortion legal.

The ruling overturned abortion laws in thirty-one states, including Texas. Fifteen states, including Georgia, would have to rewrite their more liberal laws. Three other states, Hawaii, Washington, and Alaska—where rigid abortion laws had been repealed—had residency requirements or other limits that would have to be eliminated. Only the New York law, which allowed abortion without restrictions in the first six months of pregnancy, remained unaffected by the decision.

The opinion, written by Blackmun, was a compromise of sorts. It did not grant the woman the absolute right to decide when and whether to end her pregnancy, as the *Roe* attorneys had asked. Instead, it put certain limits on abortions performed after the first three months of pregnancy.

According to the opinion, during the first three months of her pregnancy, a woman and her doctor could decide to abort "without interference by the state." Beginning with the second three months, the state could pass laws that protected the health and welfare of the mother, but not prohibit an abortion. For example, the state might regulate the qualifications of the person performing the abortion or where the abortion was to be performed. In the third three months, the states, if they chose, could ban abortion except when the mother's life was at risk.

BASED ON RIGHT TO PRIVACY

The decision noted that the Texas law violated the constitutional rights of pregnant women by violating their right to privacy. Blackmun's opinion acknowledged that the right to privacy is not explicitly mentioned in the Constitution. But, it noted, "the Court has recognized that a right of personal privacy, or a guarantee of certain areas or zones of privacy, does exist under the Constitution. . . ." The "roots" of the privacy right, according to Blackmun's opinion, are found in the First, Fourth, and Fifth amendments, in the "penumbras" (shades of meaning) of the Bill of Rights, and in the Ninth Amendment. The opinion noted that the privacy right is also found in the "concept of liberty guaranteed by the first section of the Fourteenth Amendment."

"This right of privacy, whether it be founded in the Fourteenth Amendment's concept of personal liberty and restrictions upon state action, as we feel it is, or, as the District Court determined, in the Ninth Amendment's reservation of rights to the people, is broad enough to encompass a woman's decision whether or not to terminate her pregnancy."

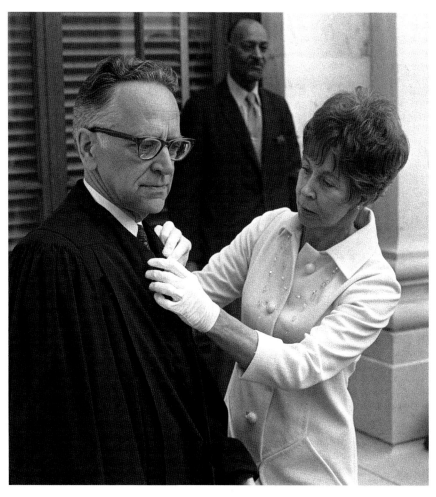

SUPREME COURT JUSTICE HARRY A. BLACKMUN WROTE THE *ROE* V. *WADE* OPINION
IN 1973. IT OVERTURNED THE BAN ON FIRST TRIMESTER ABORTIONS. HERE HE IS
PICTURED WITH HIS WIFE, WHO IS GETTING HIM READY FOR THE ANNOUNCEMENT
OF THE DECISION.

The state's interest in potential life becomes compelling enough to outweigh the right of privacy only when the fetus becomes viable, the opinion asserted. A fetus is viable when it can survive outside the mother's body. Doctors place viability at about six months, during the third term of pregnancy. With advances in medical science, however, some fetuses have been able to survive even earlier.

The opinion also agreed with Weddington's claim that Fourteenth Amendment rights apply only to persons already born, not to fetuses. The law has never recognized the unborn as living people. Since doctors, philosophers, and religious leaders cannot agree on when life begins, the opinion noted, the Court cannot be expected to provide the answer.

As in the federal court's decision, the opinion stated that John and Mary Doe had no standing to bring their case to Court. It also dismissed the claims of Dr. Hallford.

In a concurring opinion, Stewart based his reasoning on the first part of Section 1 of the Fourteenth Amendment. Abortion, he said, falls within the meaning of "liberty" as guaranteed by that clause, known as the "due process clause." Based on that clause, he noted, the Court had during the last term recognized the right of the individual to be free from "government intrusion into matters so fundamentally affecting a person as the decision whether to bear or beget a child." That right, he concluded, also includes the right of a woman to choose whether or not to end her pregnancy.

Blackmun's revised opinion had won the support of the new justice, Lewis Powell Jr. Powell had heard about the horrors of botched abortions from his father-in-law and his two brothers-in-law, all obstetricians.

In the end, Burger agreed to go with the majority.

Some believed Burger delayed his vote until after President Nixon's inauguration on January 20. It would be an embarrassment to the president that the so-called Nixon Court had struck down the abortion laws that Nixon had so vehemently supported.

"An Exercise of Raw Judicial Power"

In his dissent, White said it was up to the states to regulate abortion. He called the Court decision "an exercise of raw judicial power . . . an improvident and extravagant exercise of the power of judicial review which the Constitution extends to the Court." Rehnquist, who issued a separate dissent, questioned the right of Roe to bring the case to Court since she probably was not pregnant by then. He also argued, as White did, that the states, not the courts, should legislate abortion laws.

But Rehnquist's major difference with the decision revolved around the question of privacy. He contended

WILLIAM H. REHNQUIST DURING CONFIRMATION HEARINGS IN 1971. REHNQUIST DID NOT HEAR THE FIRST ROUND OF *ROE* ARGUMENTS. AFTER THE SECOND ARGUMENTS IN 1972, HE AND JUSTICE BYRON WHITE VOTED AGAINST *ROE*.

that an abortion could not be considered a private act, because it required an operation (outside the home). Nor, he argued, were abortions protected by the right of people "to be secure . . . in their houses . . . against unreasonable searches and seizures" as guaranteed in the Fourth Amendment. Since abortions occurred outside the home, Rehnquist argued, the state in its efforts to stop the procedure could not be accused of "seizing" a woman and invading her private property.

He also noted that the Fourteenth Amendment protected people from losing their liberty only when due process, or legal procedure, was not followed. A state, Rehnquist reasoned, could have a valid reason for limiting abortion. And, he said, it was up to Congress and state legislatures to weigh all the factors involved in the abortion question.

Rehnquist's dissent brought up many of the problems that would haunt the *Roe* decision. Constitutional scholars gave the majority opinion poor marks. They believed the Court never fully explained the concept of privacy and how it applied to abortion. In past cases, privacy had referred to private property. Police could not enter someone's private property unless they had a legal reason to do so. They had to obtain a search warrant to invade the person's privacy.

In *Roe*, privacy referred not to a secure place but to a set of personal decisions. According to *Roe*, the state could not interfere with a woman's private decision to have an abortion.

Some constitutional experts believed the decision would have been much stronger if it had been based on the *second* part of Section 1 of the Fourteenth Amendment, that read: "[States shall not] deny to any person within its jurisdiction the equal protection of the laws." They contended that bans on abortion did not treat women equally under the law. Abortion laws, they contended, interfered with women's ability to control their reproductive process. No such laws existed for men.

Blackmun's division of pregnancy into three terms raised other troubling questions. If the state had a compelling interest in preserving "potential life" in the third term, why not in the first term?

Still others objected that the abortion question should have been resolved through the democratic process, by allowing state legislators to decide the issue. The Court should not have overturned a law to enforce a right not mentioned in the Constitution, White and Rehnquist argued. Once the Court issued the *Roe* decision, legislators could no longer ban abortion.

But defenders of *Roe* argued that the right to make one's own decisions in sexual matters was a fundamental right, basic to a person's liberty. They contended that state laws interfering with such a right had to be overturned.

controversy Erupts

Reaction to the decision was quick and pointed on both sides. John Cardinal Krol of Philadelphia, president of the National Conference of Catholic Bishops, issued a statement calling the abortion ruling "an unspeakable tragedy for this nation." Terence Cardinal Cooke of New York added that the decision was "shocking and horrifying" and called the opinion a "tragic judgment." From the Vatican came a pronouncement calling it "a decision of extreme gravity that deeply affects the concepts of human life—the dignity of the human person."

On the other side, William Baird, founder of birth control clinics in New York and Massachusetts, cheered the decision. During the previous term, Baird had won his own Supreme Court case, which had overturned his conviction for distributing birth control pills. "I'm delighted to see that our position—that women have the right to control their own bodies—has been vindicated," he told *The New York Times*.

Spokespeople for the Civil Liberties Union, Protestant and Jewish organizations, and others expressed similar views. A *New York Times* editorial said the Court had "made a major contribution to the preservation of individual liberties and of free decision-making." The ruling, the editorial continued, "could bring to an end the emotional and divisive public argument over what always should have been an intensely private and personal matter." It added that the *Roe* decision provided "a sound foundation for final and reasonable resolution of a debate that has divided America too long. . . . The country will be healthier with that division ended."

Abortion rights activists assumed, like the editorial writer for *The New York Times*, that the *Roe* decision would be accepted as law. Many groups that had worked for liberalized abortion laws disbanded. Planned Parenthood and others shifted their focus to setting up abortion clinics. Now that abortion was legal, they wanted to provide low-cost, safe places where women could go for the procedure.

OPPONENTS ANSWER CALL TO ACTION

For those who opposed abortion, however, the fight was far from over. Cardinal Cooke dashed any hope that the debate would end soon when he called on Americans to "reverse this injustice to the rights of the unborn child." Many would heed the cardinal's call to action. *Roe* became a rallying cry for them.

The pro-life supporters lobbied state legislatures to pass new limits on abortion. The Catholic Church played a major role in the lobbying effort. According to records filed with the government, the Catholic Church spent $4 million lobbying Congress on the issue in 1973.

Both Catholic and Fundamentalist churches recruited new pro-life members from the pulpit. The strategy turned out to be extremely successful. Using the churches' well-established networks, the pro-life movement quickly spread nationwide.

Over the next decade, a group of prominent conservative men would shape the course of the antiabortion campaign. Howard Phillips, Paul Weyrich, Richard Viguerie, and Edward McAteer used contacts among Fundamentalist Christians to forge a new coalition of conservative groups opposed to abortion. This coalition later became known as the New Right.

Weyrich founded a group called the Free Congress Foundation, and Viguerie was publisher of the *Conservative Digest*. They joined forces with Virginia televangelist Jerry Falwell to found the Moral Majority. Their aim in creating the group was to persuade conservatives to vote, lobby, and take other political action. The fight against abortion became a prominent issue for the group.

Weyrich also urged Robert Billings to found the National Christian Action Coalition to represent conservative Christians.

Phillips, founder of yet another pro-life group

sarah standiford
Pro-Choice Activist

Sarah Standiford believes strongly in a woman's right to make her own health care choices, including the decision of whether or not to have an abortion. She worked for Planned Parenthood of Northern New England as a community relations and organizing manager for five years. In that job, she worked with women who were willing to tell their stories to help others in similar circumstances and to persuade lawmakers not to interfere with women's access to health care.

Standiford's own journey as an activist for the pro-choice cause began when she accompanied a friend to an abortion clinic. The two had been friends since their school days in Maryland. When the young woman, a college student, discovered she was pregnant, she decided to have an abortion as soon as possible. Standiford and another friend went to help her. Although abortion was legal, state regulations made it difficult for the young woman to get a first trimester abortion on her own. She decided to seek the abortion out of state.

The three young women traveled several hours to a clinic in Ohio. During the long wait before the procedure, Standiford's friend was required to attend a counseling session. Following a script dictated by state law, the counselor told the young woman of the risks posed by abortion. Standiford—noting that abortion in the first three months of a pregnancy is eleven times safer than childbirth—said the counselor exaggerated the dangers. Standiford's friend also had to look at a pamphlet that showed a fetus at various stages of development.

The abortion was performed without problems. When Standiford saw her friend in the recovery room, the friend praised the medical staff and had no complaints about the procedure. But she was distraught because she had been forced to endure barriers erected with the sole purpose of dissuading her from choosing abortion. Before coming to the clinic, the young woman had given a lot of thought to her situation and discussed her decision to have an abortion with her friends. That strangers would attempt to change her mind made her angry. She wondered if patients facing any other medical procedure had to overcome such barriers.

Her friend's experience, Standiford said, made her want to help women faced with similar barriers. Having to fight to have an abortion, she said, can make the experience much harder psychologically for women.

Although abortions remain legal throughout the United States, women may still have great difficulty getting the procedure done. Many states have imposed barriers such as waiting periods, parental notification, counseling that is biased against abortion, and other requirements designed to discourage women from having abortions. Poor women may not be able to afford the procedure, since many states and the federal government will not pay for abortions. In addition, women may have to travel for hours to reach an abortion clinic. Only 13 percent of the nation's counties have such clinics, Standiford said.

"It's an injustice that all women don't have access to health care," she said. Standiford noted that abortion-related care makes up only 5 percent of Planned

Parenthood's services but because of political pressures staff members must devote much time to testifying against bills to restrict abortions. The organization must also devote time and money to protect its staff and patients from threatened violence by abortion opponents. Since the late 1970s, family planning and abortion clinics have been the targets of 40 bombings, more than 160 arsons, and nearly 1,000 acts of vandalism. Five hundred letters falsely claiming to contain anthrax were mailed to clinics and women's rights organizations shortly after the September 11, 2001, terrorist attacks in New York and Washington, D.C.

The violence seems to be getting worse, according to the Alan Guttmacher Institute. For example, between 1991 and 1999, clinics reported more than 250 death threats. During that time, seven clinic workers were killed and thirteen wounded. In 2000, one in five clinics experienced a violent episode directed at them, according to the Feminist Majority Foundation.

Standiford shrugs off the insults hurled at her. She focuses on discussing the work of Planned Parenthood: family planning, sexuality education, cancer screening, and other health care services, in addition to abortion. Her greatest satisfaction is working with the scores of women who call the organization with thanks for making abortion and other health care services available to them. Many volunteer to tell their stories in support of Planned Parenthood. "Watching women turn their personal experiences to public actions" is Standiford's favorite part of the job.

"Being an activist means acting on my values and beliefs," Standiford said. "If I see injustice happening, I don't just sit there; I take action to make a difference. But a lone activist can only do so much. Working together we can make health care accessible to everyone."

called the Conservative Caucus, worked with Weyrich and McAteer to convince conservative Christians to become Republicans. McAteer, as national field director for the Conservative Caucus, succeeded in bringing three of the most popular televangelists—Falwell, Pat Robertson, and Jimmy Swaggart—to the Republican Party.

Before *Roe*, Republicans had led the fight for abortion reform in several states, including New York. As abortion opponents targeted their votes against liberal candidates, however, the movement began to attract support from conservative Republicans. This new coalition helped elect three conservative antiabortion presidents, Ronald Reagan in 1980 and 1984, George Bush in 1988, and George W. Bush in 2000. Reagan, despite his signing of California's liberalized abortion law in 1967, had won support from pro-life forces during his 1976 presidential run. George Bush had supported *Roe* v. *Wade* when the decision was first announced, but he changed his stand as Reagan's vice president in the early 1980s. His son, George W. Bush, allied himself early in his campaign with the antiabortion conservatives.

With a pro-life president in place in the 1980s, the movement adopted several tactics to ban abortion. In 1982 Senator Jesse Helms (R-North Carolina) introduced the Human Life Statute. The bill defined the fetus as a human being. If the bill had passed, fetuses would be entitled to the constitutional right to life. Senator Orrin Hatch (R-Utah) tried another approach. The Hatch Amendment would have given states the right to decide whether to allow abortion. Neither bill passed the Senate.

But antiabortion forces made gains on another front. Pressed by pro-lifers, state legislatures in several states passed limits on abortion. Those laws soon faced Court review. Between 1974 and 1993, the Supreme Court heard more than a dozen cases related to abortion.

Back in court

The Court in 1973 had voted by a strong majority to support abortion rights. As time went on, several of the aging justices retired. Justices appointed by antiabortion presidents, Reagan and George Bush, replaced them. The new Court still supported *Roe*, but only by a slim margin. By 1994, when Blackmun resigned, Rehnquist, a dissenter, was the only member of the *Roe* Court still on the bench.

The Court's post-*Roe* abortion decisions have been a mixed bag. In the 1976 case of *Planned Parenthood* v. *Danforth*, the Court ruled that neither husbands nor parents can veto a woman's decision to have an abortion. But the next year, the Court ruled, in *Maher* v. *Roe*, that states do not have to pay for abortions for women on welfare. In 1980, in *Harris* v. *McRae*, the Supreme Court ruled that the Hyde Amendment was constitutional. The amendment, first passed by Congress in 1976, prohibits the federal government from paying for abortions for poor women.

In other decisions, the justices ruled that:

• Doctors, not the courts, have the power to decide when a fetus might be viable. The case, *Colautti* v. *Franklin*, was decided in January 1979.

• States may require women under eighteen to get permission from their parents or from a judge for an abortion. The Court issued the decision in *Bellotti* v. *Baird* in July 1979.

Georgette Forney,
PRO-LIFE ACTIVIST

Georgette Forney got pregnant when she was sixteen. Determined to keep the unplanned pregnancy a secret from her parents, she drove herself to a Detroit clinic and had an abortion. "I remember thinking, 'This is legal, but it feels really wrong,'" she said.

Clad in a surgical gown, she joined other women in a large room, where she waited her turn. When the nurse signaled, she went into the operating room, lay on a table with her feet in stirrups, heard the whirring of a suction machine, and felt the pinching pain when it entered her body. "I felt like my soul was being taken from me," she recalled. "Even though it was my choice, I felt totally vulnerable and alone." She saw the nurse carry out a stainless-steel bowl. When she asked if it contained her baby, she was told that she would be fine. After the abortion, she spent the night at her sister's house. Her sister, her two brothers, her best friend, and her boyfriend were the only people who knew about the abortion. When she woke up the next morning, she told herself, "Yesterday never happened."

For nineteen years, Forney kept her secret—even from herself. "I never thought about it," she said. As a young

PRO-LIFE ACTIVIST GEORGETTE FORNEY IN HER OFFICE IN 2003. FORNEY, EXECUTIVE DIRECTOR OF THE NATIONAL ORGANIZATION OF EPISCOPALIANS FOR LIFE, ORGANIZED THE SILENT NO MORE CAMPAIGN IN 2002 AS A WAY TO OFFER SUPPORT TO WOMEN LIKE HERSELF WHO REGRET HAVING HAD AN ABORTION.

woman, she abused drugs and alcohol and had a number of sexual encounters. Eventually she settled down, married, and got on with her life. At first she was convinced she would never have children, a belief she later attributed to the abortion and her fear that she would be punished. Nevertheless, at twenty-eight she gave birth to a daughter, Rebekah. Although the child was healthy, Forney feared something terrible would happen to her daughter.

In 1995 Forney found her high school yearbook from the year she had had the abortion. "I had the overwhelming sense that I was holding my child," she related. "I had not allowed myself to think about it until then, but I knew instantly I had missed out on parenting a wonderful child. I began to grieve."

She confided her feelings to a friend, who advised her to attend Forgiven and Set Free, an abortion recovery group. The group helped her deal with her feelings. A friend who worked for the National Organization of Episcopalians for Life (NOEL) suggested she write about her abortion experience for a workbook the group was producing. Forney agreed as long as she would not be identified as the author. She slipped a copy of the story into her Bible, where eight-year-old Rebekah found it and read it.

Rebekah's questions poured out as the family sat eating in a local restaurant. Under her daughter's persistent cross-examination, Forney acknowledged that she had aborted her baby.

After that exchange, Forney consulted her priest for guidance. A strong pro-life advocate and the president of NOEL, he asked Forney to share her story publicly. With her daughter's encouragement, she agreed. Her priest also encouraged her to apply for the executive director post at NOEL. Until then, she had associated the pro-life cause with clinic bombings and picketing. "There was no way I was going to do that," she said.

With prayer and study, however, she realized she could make a difference in her own way. "One heart is all I need to affect," she said. In April 1998 Forney accepted the position. As NOEL's executive director, she has told her story to a national audience. Initially she feared pro-life supporters would be appalled; instead she heard from many women who shared their own stories. As an online counselor for a pregnancy center, she received e-mails from young teenaged girls who had just had an abortion and were overwhelmed and looking for help. One woman had had an abortion forty years ago and had never told anyone about it.

Forney carried her message to a 2001 candlelight vigil organized by NARAL Pro-Choice America to celebrate the anniversary of the *Roe* v. *Wade* decision. Disappointed that the pro-choice women didn't respond sympathetically to her sign, which read "I regret my abortion," she decided to organize other women with similar experiences. "That's when I really became an activist," she said. Forney organized the Silent No More campaign in 2002 with Priests for Life, a pro-life group. The group has held events in forty-six states, featuring women who talk about how abortion derailed their lives. Actress Jennifer O'Neill, who had an abortion that she later regretted, serves as the spokeswoman for the group. Her most famous movie was the 1971 drama "Summer of '42."

Forney believes society needs to provide better services for pregnant women so that they won't have to choose abortion. "Women deserve better than abortion," she said. "Our goal is not to make abortion illegal; our goal is to make abortion unthinkable."

• Abortions do not have to be performed in hospitals, according to a 1983 ruling in *Akron* v. *Akron Center for Reproductive Health*.

• Doctors do not have to tell women seeking abortions about programs to help with prenatal care and childbirth. The Court decided that case, *Thornburgh* v. *American College of Obstetricians and Gynecologists*, in June 1986.

In a split vote, the Court allowed states to place new limits on abortion in the 1989 case of *Webster* v. *Reproductive Health Services*. The ruling upheld a Missouri law that banned public money from being used for abortions. Public hospitals or staff paid by public funds could not perform abortions, according to the law. The ruling also allowed the state to require women who were at least twenty weeks pregnant to undergo tests to see if the fetus was viable. If it was, the law prohibited abortion. The Missouri law also stated that life begins at conception. But the Court chose not to rule on that portion of the law. The justices issued five separate opinions in the case.

Although the ruling did not overturn *Roe*, it put serious roadblocks in the path of any woman seeking an abortion. Spurred by the ruling, pro-choice activists began their own campaign. They worked for pro-choice candidates, promoted their cause in newspaper ads, and held rallies. A pro-choice march on Washington in 1989 drew hundreds of thousands of people.

Both sides closely watched a 1992 case, *Planned Parenthood* v. *Casey*. The case challenged a 1989 Pennsylvania law that put several restrictions on abortion. Under the law, women had to be given information provided by the state twenty-four hours before getting an abortion, minors had to have permission from a parent or guardian (or a judge's okay), and married women had to notify their husbands of their intent to get an abortion.

The eventual ruling turned out to be a confusing mix of opinions. The Court handed down two separate decisions on the case. In addition, four justices each issued separate opinions that concurred in part and dissented in part with the original decision.

The first part of the decision, supported by a 5-to-4 vote, upheld *Roe* and a woman's right to an abortion. But the decision made it clear that abortion was no longer to be considered a "fundamental" right. In a 7-to-2 vote on the second part of the decision, the Court ruled that states can impose limits on abortion as long as they do not place an "undue burden" on a woman's right to an abortion. The justices allowed all Pennsylvania's limits except the requirement that husbands be notified.

Justices Rehnquist, White, Antonin Scalia, and Clarence Thomas dissented, saying that the right to abortion is not protected by the Constitution and that *Roe* should be overruled.

Pro-lifers were incensed that the so-called conservative Rehnquist Court continued to allow abortion. Pro-choice advocates had mixed feelings about the decision. They objected that the ruling, by permitting more restrictions, prevented thousands of women from having access to abortion services. But the Court had upheld the basic right of a woman to have an abortion.

The pro-choice forces made further gains. In 1992, voters elected the pro-choice William J. Clinton as president. In one of his first acts as president, Clinton signed five decrees that eased restrictions on abortion imposed by Reagan and Bush. Pro-choice supporters lobbied to keep abortion services in Clinton's health care reform package, but Congress never approved the plan. They succeeded in winning passage of the Freedom of Access to Clinic Entrances Act. The bill, signed into law by President Clinton in May 1994, grants federal protection for women seeking abortions and clinic workers against acts of violence and terrorism.

Under the presidency of George W. Bush, pro-life supporters won several battles, including Bush's decision in July 2002 to withhold $34 million in funds from family-planning programs at the United Nations. Abortion was one of several options included in the U.N. family planning programs.

RISING VIOLENCE

Beyond the political realm, pro-life supporters continued the fight against abortion in communities throughout America. Some pro-life groups focused on peaceful protest. National Right to Life chapters organized speakers' bureaus, ad and letter-writing campaigns, and walks for life. Other groups sought to help those affected by abortion. They opened adoption clinics and offered services to unwed mothers. Georgette Forney spearheaded the Silent No More campaign to help women like herself who regretted having an abortion.

Other pro-life groups, however, became more and more aggressive. Joseph Scheidler, who founded the Pro-Life Action League in Chicago in 1980, was an early proponent of harassment and militant action against abortion clinics and their staff. He and his supporters picketed clinics, shouted at women seeking abortions, and followed clinic staff members home. Their signs carried pictures of aborted fetuses, the objects of their "rescue" attempts. John Cavanaugh-O'Keefe, known as the "father of the rescue movement," used such tactics to close more than four hundred abortion clinics.

Such protests became ever more violent. Between 1977 and 1990, more than one hundred abortion clinics were bombed or set on fire. An additional 224 were vandalized. One of the more aggressive pro-life groups, Operation Rescue, blocked clinics and prevented women from entering them. In their efforts to close clinics, more than twenty thousand Operation Rescue members had been arrested by 1989. In 1991, thousands picketed abortion clinics during an Operation Rescue protest in Wichita, Kansas, called the "Summer of Mercy." The event, planned for one week, lasted for forty-six days. The protestors directed their anger at George Tiller, a doctor who performed late-term abortions in Wichita.

Randall Terry, who founded Operation Rescue in 1986 when he was only twenty-seven, defended his group's get-tough approach to dissent. "If you think that abortion is murder," he told a local reporter, "then act like it's murder."

In response to the weeks-long protest, thousands of pro-choice activists turned out for a "Speak Out for Choice" rally in Wichita. "We're going to go toe-to-toe with these bullies," pledged Patricia Ireland, executive vice president of the National Organization for Women. The Operation Rescue protest ended with the arrest of more than 2,600 demonstrators.

In the 1990s, the violence escalated. A man wearing a ski mask fired a sawed-off shotgun at staff members

ABORTION LAWS IN THE UNITED STATES

States	'Partial-Birth' Ban	Waiting/Counseling
Alabama	Court order blocking ban	24 hours[3]
Alaska	Court order blocking ban	Counseling only
Arizona	Court order blocking ban	——
Arkansas	Court order blocking ban	At least day before
California	——	Counseling only
Colorado	——	——
Connecticut	——	Counseling only
Delaware	——	24 hours, not in effect
Florida	Court order blocking ban	Counseling, not in effect
Georgia	Meets court requirements[1]	——
Hawaii	——	——
Idaho	Court order blocking ban	24 hours
Illinois	Court order blocking ban	
Indiana	Does not meet requirements[2]	18 hours[4]
Iowa	Court order blocking ban	
Kansas	Meets court requirements[1]	24 hours
Kentucky	Court order blocking ban	24 hours
Louisiana	Court order blocking ban	24 hours[4]
Maine	——	Counseling only
Maryland	——	
Massachusetts	——	24 hours, not in effect
Michigan	Court order blocking ban	24 hours
Minnesota	——	24 hours
Mississippi	Does not meet requirements[2]	24 hours[4]
Missouri	Court order blocking ban	Counseling, not in effect
Montana	Does not meet requirements[2]	24 hours, not in effect
Nebraska	Court order blocking ban	24 hours
Nevada	——	Counseling only
New Hampshire		——
New Jersey	Court order blocking ban	——
New Mexico	Meets court requirements[1]	——
New York	——	——
North Carolina		——
North Dakota	Does not meet requirements[2]	24 hours
Ohio	Court order blocking ban	24 hours[5]
Oklahoma	Does not meet requirements[2]	——
Oregon	——	——
Pennsylvania	——	24 hours
Rhode Island	Court order blocking ban	Counseling only
South Carolina	Does not meet requirements[2]	1 hour
South Dakota	Does not meet requirements[2]	24 hours
Tennessee	Does not meet requirements[2]	48-72 hrs., not in effect
Texas	——	
Utah	Meets court requirements[1]	24 hours[4]
Vermont	——	——
Virginia	Court order blocking ban	24 hours
Washington		
West Virginia	——	24 hours
Wisconsin	Court order blocking ban	24 hours[4]
Wyoming	——	
Washington, D.C.	——	——

1 Meets the requirements set by the U.S. Supreme Court in *Stenberg* v. *Carhart*.
2 Does not meet the requirements set by the U.S. Supreme Court in *Stenberg* v. *Carhart*, but hasn't been challenged in court.
3 Waived if ectopic pregnancy or fetus has severe abnormalities. Counseling materials are not being distributed until a court reviews them.
4 Plus requires two visits to health care provider.
5 Plus requires two visits to health care provider (provision not in effect per court order).

Parental Consent	After Viability
Consent required[6]	Likely unenforceable[9]
Consent required, not in effect	—
Consent required[6]	Allows for life, health
Notification of both[6]	Allows for life, health
Consent required, not in effect	Allows for life, health
Notification only	—
No parental involvement	Allows for life, health
Notification only[6]	Not in effect
Notification required, not in effect	Likely unenforceable[9]
Notification only	Likely unenforceable[9]
No parental involvement	—
Consent required	Likely unenforceable[9]
Notification required, not in effect	Allows for life, health
Consent required	Not in effect
Notification only[6]	Likely unenforceable[9]
Notification only[6]	Allows for life, health
Consent required	Allows for life, health
Consent required	Allows for life, health
No parental involvement	Allows for life, health
Notification only[6]	Allows for life, health[10]
Consent required	Likely unenforceable[9]
Consent required	Allows for life, health
Notification only[6]	Not in effect
Consent of both parents	—
Consent required	Allows for life, health
Notification required, not in effect	Likely unenforceable[9]
Notification only[6]	Allows for life, health
Notification required, not in effect	Likely unenforceable[9]
Notification only	—
Notification required, not in effect	—
Consent required, not in effect	—
No parental involvement	Likely unenforceable[9]
Consent required[7]	Likely unenforceable[9]
Consent of both parents	Likely unenforceable[9]
Notification only[6,8]	Not in effect
Notification required, not in effect	Allows for life, health
No parental involvement	—
Consent required	Likely unenforceable[9]
Consent required	Likely unenforceable[9]
Consent required[6,7]	Likely unenforceable[9]
Notification only	Likely unenforceable[9]
Consent required[6]	Allows for life, health
Notification only	Likely unenforceable[9]
Notification only	Not in effect
No parental involvement	—
Consent required[6,7]	Likely unenforceable[9]
No parental involve.	Allows for life, health
Notification only[6]	—
Consent required[6,7]	Allows for life, health
Consent required	Likely unenforceable[9]
No parental involvement	Allows for life, health

6 A substitute can provide consent in cases of abuse, assault, incest, or neglect.

7 Allows alternate.

8 Also requires consent, but that provision is not in effect per court order.

9 Likely can't be enforced because law does not meet the requirements set down by the U.S. Supreme Court in *Roe* v. *Wade*, but hasn't been challenged in court.

10 Also for fetal abnormalities.

Source: The Alan Guttmacher Institute Web site, "State Policies in Brief," as of September 1, 2003.
http://www.agi-usa.org/pubs/spib.html

of a Springfield, Missouri, clinic in 1993. The office manager was paralyzed in the attack, and another staff member was injured.

In March of that year, Dr. David Gunn, a forty-seven-year-old doctor who performed abortions, was shot in the back three times outside his Florida clinic. He died two hours later. Michael Griffin, the thirty-one-year-old man who admitted shooting the doctor, had done volunteer work for an antiabortion group called Rescue America. Before Gunn's death, pro-life supporters had distributed wanted posters with the doctor's name and photograph on them. The following August, Tiller was shot in both arms outside his Wichita, Kansas, clinic. A pro-life demonstrator, Rachelle Renae Shannon, was charged in the shooting. The Army of God, another militant antiabortion group, uses a Web site to glorify pro-lifers jailed for violent acts, including James Kopp, accused of the 1998 killing of Dr. Barnett Slepian, who worked at an abortion clinic in Buffalo, New York.

While many pro-lifers denounced the violence, the shootings and burnings had an impact. Some clinics hired armed guards or installed security systems. Others closed. Doctors and clinic workers turned to other work rather than expose themselves and their families to danger. The closings made it increasingly difficult for women to obtain abortions. According to a survey conducted by the Alan Guttmacher Institute, an internationally known authority on sexual and reproductive health, abortion services were provided in only 13 percent of U.S. counties in 2000. In addition, a 1996 law passed by Congress allowed doctors and hospitals to refuse to perform abortions if they opposed them. This

Between 1973 and 2003, women obtained nearly 38 million abortions in the United States.

The rate of abortions in the United States peaked in 1980–1981 (at 29.3 per 1,000 women aged 15 to 44) and has declined ever since (21.3 abortions for every 1,000 women aged 15 to 44 in 2003).

Between 1994 and 2000, the rate of abortions declined by more than 10 percent. The rate among poor women, however, increased during that time.

More than half (52 percent) of women undergoing abortions are younger than twenty-five. One-third of those who get abortions are twenty to twenty-four years old.

The number of clinics and medical facilities providing abortions has declined since 1982. In 2000, there were no abortion services in 87 percent of U.S. counties, and 34 percent of American women of childbearing age lived in those counties. Fewer than half of the nation's medical schools now offer training in abortions.

Large abortion clinics (those performing 400 or more abortions) provided 93 percent of all U.S. abortions in 2000.

In 2000, 82 percent of the nation's large abortion clinics were picketed or harassed in other ways by those opposed to abortions. Picketers demonstrated at most clinics at least twenty times a year. In general, cases of more violent forms of protest, have declined since 1996.

One-quarter of U.S. pregnancies are ended by abortion. One-half of pregnancies are unplanned.

According to a 2003 Gallup Poll, 82 percent of Americans support a woman's right to an abortion if her life is endangered. Twenty-three percent of Americans believe there should be no restrictions on abortion.

In 1930, almost 2,700 American women died from abortions.

In 1950 (after the introduction of antibiotics), slightly more than three hundred women died from abortions.

In 1965, almost two hundred women died from abortions.

In 2002, three American women died from abortions. American women are eleven times more likely to die from childbirth than from abortion.

From 1972 to 1974, black and Hispanic women died from illegal abortions at a rate twelve times that for white women.

permitted hospitals throughout the country to close their facilities to women seeking abortions. In 2000, large clinics performed 93 percent of the abortions performed in the United States that year.

COURT RULINGS MIXED

Once again abortion rights groups turned to the courts to seek relief. In May 1994, a Texas jury awarded a clinic operated by Planned Parenthood of Houston and Southeast Texas $1.01 million in punitive damages from Operation Rescue and Rescue America, two antiabortion groups. Punitive damages are levied as punishment for actions done to deceive or cause injury. It was the first time a jury had required protesters to pay for damages at a clinic.

In another case, a Chicago jury ruled that the massive pro-life protests that shut down abortion clinics in the 1980s and early 1990s amounted to extortion. The jury awarded damages of $258,000 to abortion clinics and their patients, represented by the National Organization for Women (NOW), and ordered payment from Scheidler's Pro-Life Action Network, a coalition of antiabortion groups that included Operation Rescue. The court cases led to the disbanding of Operation Rescue, which later re-formed into Operation Save America.

In February 2003 the Supreme Court overturned the verdict in the NOW case. In an eight-to-one vote, the Court ruled that because the protestors did not profit from their actions, they could not be guilty of extortion. Free speech advocates—including some abortion rights supporters—hailed the decision. But some pro-choice groups worried that the decision might encourage renewed violence. Since the late 1990s, acts of violence at abortion clinics have decreased, although antiabortion groups still picket. They also continue to use national advertising campaigns and political contributions to further their cause.

In 2000, an estimated 1.31 million women had abortions. A majority of them were unmarried and in their twenties. Better access to birth control, education on birth control as well as an emphasis on abstaining from sex, a decline in the birth rate, and more tolerance for unmarried mothers have all been credited for the decrease in abortions. While the abortion rate is decreasing overall, the rate of abortions among poor women began rising sharply in 1994. Part of the problem, say clinic workers, is that poor women do not have access to birth control methods.

Medical advances in recent years have also played a role in reducing the number of abortions. The so-called abortion pill, RU-486 (mifepristone), has allowed some women to have abortions without surgery. The pill, a hormone, interferes with the woman's hormones and causes the body to abort the fetus. The U.S. government approved the pill in 2000 for use during the first seven weeks of pregnancy. In less than a year, 37,000 women had used it to abort pregnancies. The pill could make it easier for women to obtain abortions earlier if general doctors outside of clinics prescribe it.

Women are also using emergency contraception—taking an extra dose of birth control pills within 72 hours of unprotected sex. The pills can prevent an egg from being fertilized or from developing into a fetus. The Alan Guttmacher Institute estimates emergency contraception prevented more than 51,000 abortions in 2000.

ROE'S FUTURE?

Roe v. *Wade* brought the explosive issue of abortion to the forefront. After three decades of court fights, legislative battles, and fierce protests, the issue remains unresolved. The two sides of the issue may never be able to find common ground. At one end of the scale are those who believe abortion is murder. At the other are those who believe the woman—and she alone—should have the right to decide whether to have an abortion.

In the thirty-one years since the Supreme Court issued its decision in the *Roe* case, new laws on both the state and national level have chipped away at abortion rights. Many states now require teens to get permission from one or both parents (or a judge) before getting an abortion. The Supreme Court has upheld laws that ban public funding of abortions and require counseling before women can obtain abortions. These laws make it more difficult for poor women and teens to get abortions and in some cases force women to delay the procedure. In addition, the federal ban on payment for abortions limits access for all women who work for the federal government, including those in the military, Peace Corps volunteers, women in prison, and those who depend on Medicaid for health care.

Thirteen states limit insurance coverage for abortions, in some cases banning it altogether except when the mother's life is in danger.

In November 2003, Congress passed and President George W. Bush signed into law a bill that banned a procedure that has been called a partial-birth abortion. It was the first time the federal government had banned a specific abortion procedure since *Roe*. Thirty-one states already had laws that banned the procedure. The federal law and most of the state laws allowed partial-birth abortions only if the mother's life is in danger.

The term "partial-birth abortion" presumably refers to a procedure doctors call "intact dilation and extraction" (D&X). As defined by the American College of Obstetricians and Gynecologists (ACOG), the procedure collapses the skull of the fetus and then removes it through the mother's vagina. It is used, according to doctors, when a continued pregnancy poses a severe threat to the mother, the fetus is severely deformed, or both. The procedure is extremely rare. In 2000, fewer than two-tenths of one percent (.17 percent) of all abortions involved D&Xs, according to researchers. A survey conducted by the Alan Guttmacher Institute concluded that most D&X procedures were performed when the mother was in the twentieth to twenty-fourth week of pregnancy (4.6 to 5.5 months). Only 1 percent of all U.S. abortions occur after the twentieth week of pregnancy, according to the Institute.

The federal law, called the Partial-Birth Abortion Ban Act of 2003, defined the procedure as a vaginal delivery of a living fetus "for the purpose of performing an overt act that the person knows will kill the partially delivered living fetus." The law made no mention of the stage of pregnancy or the exact "overt act" used.

Controversy swirled around efforts to ban partial-birth abortions for at least ten years before the bill's passage. Congress twice passed bills to ban the procedure during Bill Clinton's presidency, but Clinton vetoed both measures.

Pro-life supporters, who termed the procedure "brutal" and "barbaric," praised the law and said it would save lives. The law's opponents charged that it deprived women of access to the best health care available and prevented doctors from using their own judgment in treating patients. The ACOG, which advises doctors against using the procedure, nevertheless opposed the bill, which the group said "would supersede the medical judgment of a trained physician, in consultation with a patient, as to what is the safest and most appropriate medical procedure for that particular patient." Doctors could be jailed for up to two years for violating the ban. The doctors' group also noted that the law could outlaw other abortion methods that were "critical to the lives and health of American women."

Even before President Bush signed the bill, several pro-choice groups, including Planned Parenthood and the National Abortion Federation, filed suit to block the law. They argued that the law was unconstitutional because it made no exception when a woman's health was threatened. They also noted that the law's definition of the procedure was too vague and could be applied to abortions performed at any stage of pregnancy.

Just after Bush signed the bill into law, a federal judge in Manhattan blocked the ban, granting a temporary restraining order to the National Abortion Federation, a network of abortion providers that had challenged the act as unconstitutional. That network has clinics in all but three states and treats 700,000 women a year, so the effect of the temporary restraining order was expected to have national implications.

A 2000 Supreme Court ruling on a Nebraska law struck down a similar partial-birth abortion ban in that state, but the ruling applied only to the four doctors bringing the lawsuit. In *Stenberg* v. *Carhart*, the Supreme Court ruled against Nebraska's ban because it was too restrictive (it did not allow abortions if the mother's health was endangered) and because the law was too vague. The ruling came on a 5-to-4 vote. Some observers believe *Roe* will be overturned when one of the five justices voting in the majority retires—or before.

Those who oppose abortion continue to search for a case that will win the support of the majority and overturn *Roe*. They hoped that a case filed by Norma McCorvey, the original Jane Roe, would be such a case. McCorvey filed suit in June 2003 asking the Court to reverse the decision that made her famous. Now an antiabortion activist, McCorvey presented testimony from more than one thousand women who said abortions had harmed them. A federal district court judge dismissed the suit later that month, ruling that it had not been filed within a "reasonable time."

Marvin Olasky, a conservative writer, believes that Americans are rethinking their support of abortion. The Court, he contends, will eventually respond by overturning *Roe*, as the Court overturned *Plessy* v. *Ferguson*, the 1896 case that approved racial segregation. "That took sixty years," Olasky said. "We're halfway there."

Other observers, however, note that the Court—not even the Rehnquist Court with six of its nine members appointed by conservative, antiabortion presidents—seldom overturns well-established rulings. And, they point out, Americans still overwhelmingly support legal abortion. According to polls conducted by the *Wall Street Journal* and NBC News, support for abortion has changed little in the past dozen years. In January 2003, 59 percent of Americans said they thought the decision on whether to have an abortion should be made by the woman and her doctor. In July 1990, 57 percent agreed with the position. Only 9 percent in 2003 and 8 percent in 1990 believed abortion should always be illegal. Another 29 percent in 2003 and 33 percent in 1990 said abortion should be allowed only in the case of rape or incest or when the woman's life was in danger.

The major tenet of the *Roe* decision remains. A woman has a right, protected by the Constitution, to have an abortion if she chooses. The government cannot require undue burdens of a woman that interfere with that right. The fact that the decision still stands is a testament to the strength of the Supreme Court and of the Constitution.

NOTES

Chapter 1

pp. 11–12, Angela Bonavoglia, ed. *The Choices We Made: Twenty-Five Women and Men Speak Out About Abortion*. New York: Random House, 1991.

p. 12, par. 3, Alfred C. Kinsey. *Sexual Behavior in the Human Female*. Philadelphia: W.B. Saunders, 1953.

p. 12, par. 4, Marian Faux. *Crusaders: Voices from the Abortion Front*. New York: Birch Lane Press, 1990.

p. 15, par. 5, Sherri Finkbine. "The Lesser of Two Evils," *The Case for Legalized Abortion*, ed. Alan F. Guttmacher, M.D. Berkeley, CA: Diablo Press, 1967.

p. 16, par. 4, *The New York Times*, July 25, 1962, p. 22.

p. 17, par. 2, Sherri Finkbine. "The Lesser of Two Evils."

p. 17, par. 3, *The New York Times*, July 31,1962, p. 9.

p. 17, par. 5, *The New York Times*, Aug. 1, 1962, p. 19.

p. 18, par. 3–5, *The New York Times*, Aug. 4, 1962, p. 20.

p. 20, par. 3, *The New York Times*, Aug. 18, 1962, p. 43.

p. 20, par. 4, *The New York Times*, Aug. 27, 1962, p. 20.

p. 20, par. 5, Sherri Finkbine. "The Lesser of Two Evils."

Chapter 2

p. 22, par. 3; p. 23, par. 1–3; p. 24, par. 3–4; p. 25, par. 1, Laurence H. Tribe. *Abortion: The Clash of Absolutes*. New York: W. W. Norton & Co., 1992.

p. 24, par. 1, American Medical Association report, 1871.

p. 24, par. 2, Comstock Act of 1873.

p. 26, par. 4; p. 27, par. 1, *The New York Times*, Jan. 31, 1965, p. 73.

p. 27, par. 2; p. 28, par. 1, *The New York Times*, Jan. 26, 1967, p. 18.

p. 28, par. 1, *The New York Times*, Feb. 13, 1967, p. 1.

p. 28, par. 2, Sarah Weddington. *A Question of Choice.* New York: G. P. Putnam's Sons, 1992.

p. 28, par. 2, *The New York Times*, Jan. 18, 1967, p. 14.

p. 28, par. 4, *The New York Times*, May 22, 1967, p.1.

p. 29, par. 1–3, "Mrs. X." "One Woman's Abortion," *Atlantic Monthly*, August 1965
http://www.theatlantic.com/politics/abortion/mrsx.htm

p. 30, par. 1, *The New York Times*, June 22, 1967, p. 1.

p. 30, par. 4; p. 32, par. 1, Laura Kaplan. *The Story of Jane: The Legendary Underground Feminist Abortion Service.* Chicago: University of Chicago Press, 1997.

p. 33, par. 2, *The New York Times*, June 16, 1967, p. 24.

p. 33, par. 3; p. 35, par. 1, Laurence H. Tribe. *Abortion: The Clash of Absolutes.*

p. 35, par. 3, Dorothy Fadiman. *From Danger to Dignity: The Fight for Safe Abortion.* Documentary film produced by Concentric Media in collaboration with KTEH-TV, 1995
http://www.concentric.org/projects/danger.html

pp. 36–39, from author's interviews with Lee Michaels, June 30, and July 2, 2003.

p. 36, par. 3, Bill Kovach. "Assembly Passes Abortion Bill," *The New York Times*, April 10, 1970.

p. 40, par. 3, National Right to Life Committee, Pennsylvania
http://www.pennlife.org/docs/abort_history.html

p. 40, par. 4, "Vatican/Abortion," CBS Evening News with Walter Cronkite, Oct. 12, 1970.

p. 41, par. 3, *United States* v. *Vuitch*, 305 F. Supp. 1032 (DC 1969)
http://members.aol.com/abtrbng/vuitchdist.htm

p. 42, par. 1, *Abramowicz* v. *Lefkowitz*, 67 Civ. 4469 (S.D.N.Y.).

Chapter 3

p. 43, par. 2, Dana Rubin, "Roe Redux," *Texas Monthly*, vol. 21, February 1993, p. 185.

p. 43, par. 3; p. 45, par. 1, Sarah Weddington. *A Question of Choice*. New York: G. P. Putnam's Sons, 1992.

p. 45, par. 2, *Griswold* v. *Connecticut*, 381 US 479 (1965) http://www.findlaw.com/casecode/supreme.html

p. 45, par. 2, Fourteenth Amendment, U.S. Constitution.

p. 46, par. 2–4, *People* v. *Belous*, 458 P.2d 194 (Cal. 1969) http://caselaw.lp.findlaw.com/ca/cal2d/year/1969_9.html

pp. 47–48; p. 51, par. 1, Sarah Weddington, *A Question of Choice*.

p. 51, par. 1, *The New York Times*, Sept. 9, 1987, p. 23.

Chapter 4

p. 54, par. 3–4, Sarah Weddington. *A Question of Choice*. New York: G. P. Putnam's Sons, 1992.

pp. 55–57, The Supreme Court Historical Society http://www.supremecourthistory.org Administrative Office of the U.S. Courts, http://www.uscourts.gov Iowa Court Information System http://www.judicial.state.ia.us/students/6

p. 58, par. 1–2, Marian Faux. Roe *v.* Wade: *The Untold Story of the Landmark Supreme Court Decision That Made Abortion Legal*. New York: Penguin Books, 1993.

p. 58, par. 3; p. 61, par. 5, Sarah Weddington. *A Question of Choice*.

p. 63, par. 4, Marian Faux. *Roe* v. *Wade*.

Chapter 5

p. 67, par. 1–p. 69, par. 3; p. 70, par. 1, 3; p. 71, par. 3, Sarah Weddington. *A Question of Choice*, New York: G. P. Putnam's Sons, 1992.

p. 69, par. 3, Plaintiff's Brief, *Roe* v. *Wade*.

p. 72, par. 1–3, "Norma McCorvey (alias Jane Roe)" in *The Choices We Made: Twenty-Five Women Speak Out about Abortion*, ed. Angela Bonavoglia. New York: Random House, 1991.

p. 73, par. 1, "Lawyer, 'Roe' Now at Odds on Abortion," The Associated Press, *The New York Times*, Jan. 21, 2003.

p. 73, par. 4–p. 74, par.2, Norma McCorvey with Gary Thomas. *Won By Love: Norma McCorvey, Jane Roe of Roe v. Wade, Speaks Out for the Unborn As She Shares Her New Conviction for Life*. Nashville, TN: Thomas Nelson Publishers, 1998.

p. 74, par. 3, Lisa Falkenberg. "Court dismisses McCorvey's request to reopen *Roe* v. *Wade*," Associated Press, June 20, 2003.

p. 74, par. 4, Norma McCorvey, Roe No More Ministry http://www.roenomore.org

p. 75, par. 1–p. 76, par. 2, Sarah Weddington. *A Question of Choice.*

p. 76, par. 3, Bob Woodward and Scott Armstrong. *The Brethren: Inside the Supreme Court*. New York: Simon and Schuster, 1979.

Chapter 6

p. 79, par. 1, 3, Sarah Weddington. *A Question of Choice*. New York: G. P. Putnam's Sons, 1992.

p. 80, par. 4–p. 83, par. 7, Transcript of oral arguments, *Roe* v. *Wade*, Dec. 13, 1971.

p. 85, par. 3–p. 87, par. 1, Bob Woodward and Scott Armstrong. *The Brethren: Inside the Supreme Court*. New York: Simon and Schuster, 1979.

p. 88, par. 1, *The New York Times*, May 14, 1972, p. 1.

p. 89, par. 5, *Morning Edition*, National Public Radio, Aug. 31, 1993 http://www.npr.org/transcripts/seriesedit.html

p. 90–91, Transcript of oral arguments, *Roe* v. *Wade*, Oct. 11, 1972.

Chapter 7

p. 94, par. 1–p. 96, par. 3, *Roe v. Wade*, 410 U.S. 113 (1973)
http://www.findlaw.com/casecode/supreme.html

p. 96, par. 4, concurring opinion, Potter Stewart, *Roe v. Wade*.

p. 96–97, par. 5–6, p. 97, par. 1, Bob Woodward and Scott Armstrong. *The Brethren: Inside the Supreme Court*. New York:Simon and Schuster, 1979.

p. 97, par. 2, dissent, Byron White, *Roe v. Wade*.

p. 97, par. 2–p. 98, par. 2, dissent, William Rehnquist, *Roe v. Wade*.

p. 98, par. 3–p. 99, par. 3, Kermit L. Hall, ed. *The Oxford Companion to the Supreme Court of the United States*. New York: Oxford University Press, 1992.

p. 99, par. 5–p. 100, par. 2. *The New York Times*, Jan. 23, 1973, p. 1.

p. 101, par. 1, Laurence H. Tribe. *Abortion: The Clash of Absolutes*. New York: W. W. Norton & Co., 1992.

p. 101, par. 3–6, Pam Chamberlain and Jean Hardisty. "Reproducing Patriarchy: Reproductive Rights Under Siege," *The Public Eye Magazine*
http://www.publiceye.org/magazine/v14n1/ReproPatriarch–05.htm

pp. 102–104, author's interview with Sarah Standiford, July 16, 2003.

p. 106, par. 2, *Planned Parenthood of Central Missouri* v. *Danforth*, 428 US 52 (1976)
http://www.findlaw.com/casecode/supreme.html

p. 106, par. 2, *Maher* v. *Roe*, 432 US 464 (1977)
http://www.findlaw.com/casecode/supreme.html

p. 106, par. 2, *Harris* v. *McRae*, 448 US 297 (1980)
http://www.findlaw.com/casecode/supreme.html

p. 106, par. 3, *Colautti* v. *Franklin*, 439 US 379 (1979)
http://www.findlaw.com/casecode/supreme.html

p. 106, par. 4, *Bellotti* v. *Baird*, 443 US 622 (1979)
http://www.findlaw.com/casecode/supreme.html

p. 107–109, author's interview with Georgette Forney, July 16, 2003.

p. 110, par. 1, *Akron* v. *Akron Center for Reproductive Health*, 462 US 416 (1983)
http://www.findlaw.com/casecode/supreme.html

p. 110, par. 2, *Thornburgh* v. *American College of Obstetricians and Gynecologists*, 476 US 747 (1986)
http://www.findlaw.com/casecode/supreme.html

p. 110, par. 3, *Webster* v. *Reproductive Health Services*, 462 US 416, 444 (1983)
http://www.findlaw.com/casecode/supreme.html

p. 110, par. 5–p. 111, par. 3, *Planned Parenthood* v. *Casey*, 505 US 833 (1992)
http://www.findlaw.com/casecode/supreme.html

p. 112, par. 1, "Family Unplanning," *The New York Times*, July 28, 2002, Sect. 4, p. 2.

p. 112, par. 3, Pam Chamberlain and Jean Hardisty. "Reproducing Patriarchy: Reproductive Rights Under Siege."

p. 112, par. 4–p. 113, par. 2, Laurence H. Tribe. *Abortion: The Clash of Absolutes*.

p. 113, par. 1–2, Judy Lundstrom Thomas. "Terry and His Cause Allow No Neutrality," *The Wichita Eagle*, Aug. 25, 1991, p. 1A.

p. 113, par. 4, Hurst Laviana and Bud Norman. "Abortion-Rights Rally Sends a Loud Message," *The Wichita Eagle*, Aug. 25, 1991, p. 1A.

p. 116, par. 1, "Thou Shalt Not Kill," *Time*, vol. 141, No. 12, March 22, 1993.

p. 116, par. 1, "Rising Tide of Zealotry/Abortion: Violence May Split the Pro-Life Forces," *Newsweek*, vol. CXXII, No. 9, Aug. 30, 1993.

p. 116, par. 1, Army of God Web site
http://www.armyofgod.com, accessed June 23, 2003.

p. 116, par. 2, The Alan Guttmacher Institute Web site
http://www.agi-usa.org

p. 117, Linda Feldmann. "The Abortion Wars: 30 Years after *Roe* v. *Wade*," *Christian Science Monitor*, Jan. 22, 2003.
National Vital Statistics Reports (50, 23).
The Alan Guttmacher Institute Web site,
http://www.agi-usa.org

Adrienne Washington. "30 Years Later, Still No Truce in the Abortion Conflict," *The Washington Times*, Jan. 24, 2003.

Donald Lambro. "Pro-choicers Celebrate *Roe*, Concede Gains by Opponents," *The Washington Times*, Jan. 22, 2003.

p. 118, par. 2, *National Organization for Women, Inc., et al. v. Scheidler et al.*, 510 US 249 (1994).
http://www.findlaw.com/casecode/supreme.html

p. 118, par. 3, *Joseph Scheidler, Andrew Scholberg, Timothy Murphy, and The Pro-Life Action League, Inc. v. National Organization for Women, Inc., et al.*, No. 01–1118 (2003)
http://caselaw.lp.findlaw.com/scripts/
getcase.pl?court=US&vol=000&invol=01-1118

p. 119, par. 1–3; p. 120, par. 2–3, The Alan Guttmacher Institute Web site
http://www.agi-usa.org/pubs/spib.html

p. 120, par. 3, The Alan Guttmacher Institute Web site, "State Policies in Brief: Restricting Insurance Coverage of Abortion," Jan. 1, 2004
http://www.guttmacher.org/pubs/spib.html

p. 120, par. 4–p. 121, par. 2, Andis Robexnieks. "Ban on Intact Dilatation and Extraction Passes in the Senate," *American Medical News*, April 7, 2003
http://www.ama-assn.org/amed-news/2003/04/07/
prsco407.htm

p. 120, par. 4, The Alan Guttmacher Institute Web site, "State Policies in Brief: Bans on 'Partial-Birth' Abortion," Jan. 1, 2004
http://www.guttmacher.org/pubs/spib.html

p. 121, par. 1, American College of Obstetricians and Gynecologists. "Statement on So-Called 'Partial Birth Abortion' Laws," February 13, 2002
http://www.acog.org/from_home/publications/
press_releases/nr02-13-02.cfm

p. 121, par. 1, Andis Robexnieks. "Ban on Intact Dilatation and Extraction Passes in the Senate," *American Medical News*, April 7, 2003

http://www.ama-assn.org/amednews/
2003/04/07/prsc0407.htm

p. 121, par. 1, "Abortion Incidence and Services in the
United States in 2000," Alan Guttmacher Institute,
Perspectives on Sexual and Reproductive Health,
Jan./Feb
http://www.agi-usa.org/pubs/journals/3500603.pdf

p. 121, par. 2; p. 122, par. 1, Sheryl Gay Stolberg.
"Senate Approves Bill to Prohibit Type of Abortion,"
The New York Times, Oct. 22, 2003

p. 121, par. 3, Sheryl Gay Stolberg. "Senate Approves
Bill to Prohibit Type of Abortion," *The New York Times*,
Oct. 22, 2003.

p. 122, par. 1, American College of Obstetricians and
Gynecologists. "Statement on So-Called 'Partial Birth
Abortion' Laws," February 13, 2002.
http://www.acog.org/from_home/publications/
press_releases/nr02-13-02.cfm

p. 122, par. 3, Susan Saulny. "Court Blocks New
Statute That Limits Abortions," *The New York Times*,
November 7, 2003.

p. 122, par. 3, *Stenberg* v. *Carhart*, 530 US 914 (2000)
http://www.findlaw.com/casecode/supreme.html

p. 123, par. 2, Lisa Falkenberg. "Court Dismisses
McCorvey's Request to Reopen *Roe* v. *Wade*," Associated
Press, June 20, 2003.

p. 123, par. 3, Linda Feldmann. "The Abortion Wars: 30
Years after *Roe* v. *Wade*," *Christian Science Monitor*, Jan.
22, 2003.

p. 123, par. 3–p.124, par. 1, NBC News/*Wall Street Journal* poll
conducted by the polling organizations of Peter Hart
(D) and Robert Teeter (R), Jan. 19–21, 2003
http://www.pollingreport.com/abortion.htm

furTHer informaTion

BOOKS

Cornelius, Kay. *The Supreme Court* (Your Government: How It Works). Broomall, PA: Chelsea House Publishers, 2000.

Emmens, Carol. *The Abortion Controversy*, rev. ed. New York: Julian Messner, 1992.

Guernsey, Joann Bren. *Abortion: Understanding the Controversy (Pro/Con)*. Minneapolis, MN: Lerner Publications Co., 1993.

Heath, David, and Charlotte Wilcox. *The Supreme Court of the United States* (American Civics). Mankato, MN: Bridgestone Books, 1999.

Hull, N. E. H., and Peter Charles Hoffer. Roe *v.* Wade: *The Abortion Rights Controversy in American History (Landmark Law Cases and American Society)*. Lawrence: University Press of Kansas, 2001.

Levert, Suzanne. *The Supreme Court*. New York: Benchmark Books, 2002.

McCorvey, Norma, and Gary Thomas. *Won by Love: Norma McCorvey, Jane Roe of Roe v. Wade, Speaks Out for the Unborn As She Shares Her New Conviction for Life*. Nashville, TN: Thomas Nelson Publishers, 1998.

Patrick, John J. *The Supreme Court of the United States: A Student Companion (Oxford Student Companions to American Government)*, second ed. New York: Oxford University Press Children's Books, 2002.

Reagan, Leslie J. *When Abortion Was a Crime: Women, Medicine, and Law in the United States, 1867–1973*. Los Angeles: University of California Press, 1997.

Roleff, Tamara L. *Abortion: Opposing Viewpoints* (Opposing Viewpoints Series). San Diego: Greenhaven Press, 1997.

Sanders, Mark C. *Supreme Court* (American Government Today Series). Austin, TX: Raintree/Steck-Vaughn Publishers, 2001.

Solinger, Rickie. *Abortion Wars: A Half Century of Struggle, 1950–2000*. Los Angeles: University of California Press, 1998.

Weddington, Sarah. *A Question of Choice*. New York: G. P. Putnam's Sons, 1992.

Web Sites
The Alan Guttmacher Institute
http://www.agi-usa.org

"American Memory," Historical Collections for the National Digital Library, Library of Congress
http://memory.loc.gov

Constitutional Law Foundation
http://www.conlaw.org/cites2.htm
Library of Congress
http://www.loc.gov/rr/mss/blackmun

NARAL Pro-Choice America
http://www.naral.org
National Public Radio
http://www.npr.org/news/specials/blackmun

National Right to Life Committee
http://www.nrlc.org

National Silent No More Awareness Campaign
http://www.silentnomoreawareness.org/

Our Bodies Ourselves, the Boston Women's Health Book Collective
http://www.ourbodiesourselves.org/abortion.htm

Oyez Project: U.S. Supreme Court Multimedia
http://www.oyez.org/oyez/frontpage

Planned Parenthood Federation of America Inc.
http://www.plannedparenthood.org/

Roe No More Ministry, Norma McCorvey
http://www.roenomore.org

Supreme Court Historical Society
http://www.supremecourthistory.org

BIBLIOGRAPHY

Bonavoglia, Angela, ed. *The Choices We Made: Twenty-Five Women and Men Speak Out About Abortion*. New York: Random House, 1991.

Dorf, Michael C. "The Thirtieth Anniversary of *Roe* v. *Wade*: Was It Rightly Decided? Will It Be Overruled?" http://writ.corporate.findlaw.com/dorf/20030122.html

Fadiman, Dorothy. *From Danger to Dignity: The Fight for Safe Abortion*. Documentary film produced by Concentric Media in collaboration with KTEH-TV, 1995. http://www.concentric.org/projects/danger.html

Falkenberg, Lisa. "Court dismisses McCorvey's request to reopen *Roe* v. *Wade*." Associated Press (June 20, 2003).

Faux, Marian. *Crusaders: Voices from the Abortion Front*. New York: Birch Lane Press, 1990.

———. Roe *v.* Wade: *The Untold Story of the Landmark Supreme Court Decision That Made Abortion Legal*, New York: Penguin Books, 1993.

Feldmann, Linda. "The Abortion Wars: 30 Years After *Roe* v. *Wade*." *Christian Science Monitor* (Jan. 22, 2003).

Finkbine, Sherri. "The Lesser of Two Evils," *The Case for Legalized Abortion*, ed. Alan F. Guttmacher, M.D. Berkeley, CA: Diablo Press, 1967.

Hall, Kermit L., ed. *The Oxford Companion to the Supreme Court of the United States.* New York: Oxford University Press, 1992.

Kaplan, Laura. *The Story of Jane: The Legendary Underground Feminist Abortion Service.* Chicago: University of Chicago Press, 1997.

Kinsey, Alfred C., et al. *Sexual Behavior in the Human Female.* Philadelphia: W. B. Saunders, 1953.

McCorvey, Norma, and Gary Thomas. *Won by Love: Norma McCorvey, Jane Roe of Roe v. Wade, Speaks Out for the Unborn As She Shares Her New Conviction for Life.* Nashville, TN: Thomas Nelson Publishers, 1998.

"Morning Edition," *National Public Radio*, August 31, 1993. http://www.npr.org/transcripts/seriesedit.html

"Mrs. X." "One Woman's Abortion." *Atlantic Monthly*, August 1965.
http//:www.theatlantic.com/politics/abortion/mrsx.htm

Reagan, Leslie J. *When Abortion Was a Crime: Women, Medicine, and Law in the United States, 1867–1973.* Los Angeles: University of California Press, 1997.

"Rising Tide of Zealotry/Abortion: Violence May Split the Pro-Life Forces," *Newsweek*, vol. CXXII, no. 9. (August 30, 1993).

Rubin, Dana. "Roe Redux," *Texas Monthly*, vol. 21. (February 1993).

Smolowe, Jill. "New, Improved and Ready for Battle," *Time*, vol. 141, no. 24. (June 14, 1993).

Solinger, Rickie. *Abortion Wars: A Half Century of Struggle, 1950–2000*. Los Angeles: University of California Press, 1998.

"30th Anniversary of *Roe* v. *Wade*: NPR News Series Examines Landmark Abortion Ruling." (January 21, 2003). http://www.npr.org/news/specials/roevwade/index.html

"Thou Shalt Not Kill," *Time*, vol. 141, no. 12. (March 22, 1993).

Tribe, Laurence H. *Abortion: The Clash of Absolutes*. New York: W. W. Norton & Co., 1992.

Weddington, Sarah. *A Question of Choice*. New York: G. P. Putnam's Sons, 1992.

Woodward, Bob, and Scott Armstrong. *The Brethren: Inside the Supreme Court*. New York: Simon and Schuster, 1979.

Zernike, Kate. "30 Years After *Roe* v. *Wade*, New Trends but the Old Debate." *The New York Times* (January 20, 2003).

STATUTES/COURT CASES/DOCUMENTS

Abramowicz v. Lefkowitz, 67 Civ. 4469 (S.D.N.Y.).

Akron v. Akron Center for Reproductive Health, 462 US 416 (1983).

Bellotti v. Baird, 443 US 622 (1979).

Board of Regents v. Roth, 408 US 564 (1972).

Colautti v. Franklin, 439 US 379 (1979).

Doe v. Bolton, 410 U.S. 179 (1973).

Griswold et al. v. Connecticut, 381 US 479 (1965).

Harris v. McRae, 448 US 297 (1980).

Maher v. Roe, 432 US 464 (1977).

National Organization for Women, Inc., et al. v. Scheidler et al., 510 US 249 (1994).

People v. Belous, 458 P.2d 194 (Cal. 1969).

Planned Parenthood of Central Missouri v. Danforth, 428 US 52 (1976).

Planned Parenthood v. Casey, 505 US 833 (1992).

Roe v. Wade, 410 U.S. 113 (1973).

Joseph Scheidler, Andrew Scholberg, Timothy Murphy, and The Pro-Life Action League, Inc. v. National Organization for Women, Inc., et al., No. 01-1118 (2003).

Stenberg v. Carhart, 530 US 914 (2000).

Thornburgh v. American College of Obstetricians and Gynecologists, 476 US 747 (1986).

United States v. Vuitch, 305 F.Supp. 1032 (DC 1969).

Webster v. Reproductive Health Services, 462 US 416, 444 (1983).

First, Third, Fourth, Fifth, Eighth, Ninth, and Fourteenth amendments, U.S. Constitution.

index

Page numbers in **boldface** are illustrations, tables, and charts

about the author

SUSAN DUDLEY GOLD has written more than three dozen books for middle-school and high-school students on a variety of topics, including American history, health issues, law, and space. Her most recent works for Benchmark Books are *Gun Control* in the Open for Debate series, and *Roe v. Wade: A Woman's Choice?*, *Brown v. Board of Education: Separate but Equal?*, and *The Pentagon Papers: National Security or the Right to Know?*—all in the Supreme Court Milestones series. She is currently working on two more books about Supreme Court cases.

Susan Gold has also written several books on Maine history. Among her many careers in journalism are stints as a reporter for a daily newspaper, managing editor of two statewide business magazines, and free-lance writer for several regional publications. She and her husband, John Gold, own and operate a Web design and publishing business. Susan has received numerous awards for her writing and design work. In 2001 she received a Jefferson Award for community service in recognition of her work with a support group for people with chronic pain, which she founded in 1993. Susan and her husband, also a children's book author, live in Maine. They have one son, Samuel.